MOUNTAIN MAN SKILLS

MOUNTAIN MAN SKILLS

HUNTING, TRAPPING, WOODWORK, AND MORE

Edited by Stephen Brennan

SKYHORSE PUBLISHING

Skyhorse Publishing books may be purchased in bulk at special discounts for sales promotion, corporate gifts, fund-raising, or educational purposes. Special editions can also be created to specifications. For details, contact the Special Sales Department, Skyhorse Publishing, 307 West 36th Street, 11th Floor, New York, NY 10018 or info@skyhorsepublishing.com.

Skyhorse® and Skyhorse Publishing® are registered trademarks of Skyhorse Publishing, Inc.®, a Delaware corporation.

Visit our website at www.skyhorsepublishing.com.

10 9 8 7

Library of Congress Cataloging-in-Publication Data is available on file.

Cover design by Jane Sheppard
Cover photos: ThinkStock

Print ISBN: 978-1-62873-709-7
Ebook ISBN: 978-1-62914-049-0

Printed in China

MOUNTAIN MAN SKILLS

CONTENTS

MOUNTAIN MAN SKILLS

The evolution of the trapper may be traced back to the old French régime when the *coureurs des bois*, rangers of the woods, or the peddlers of the wilderness, held sway. These were, however, more traders than trappers, purchasing the pelts from the Indians for trifles and frequently accompanying them on their hunting excursions. They were as profligate as their successors, and their occupation passed away with the passing of the French control of Canada and with the establishment of the interior trading-posts by the merchants of Canada, who later formed companies and conducted the business in a more systematic manner. From these interior trading-posts. traders and trappers were sent out to trade with the Indians and trap in their territory at the same time. The trading gradually fell into the hands of the trading-posts; the trapper meanwhile pursued his vocation, and it became his recognized and established business, where he remained an important factor in the fur-trade down to the time of its decline and ultimate death.

While Mr. Hunt was at Mackinaw engaging men for the Astoria venture, there arrived at this place some of these characters, and his description of them is so accurate that I take the liberty of giving it here:

> A chance party of "Northwesters" appeared at Mackinaw from the rendezvous at Fort William. These held themselves up as the chivalry of the fur-trade. They were

men of iron; proof against cold weather, hard fare, and perils of all kinds. Some would wear the Northwest button, and a formidable dirk, and assume something of a military air. They generally wore feathers in their hats, and affected the "brave." "Je suis un homme du nord!" "I am a man of the north"—one of these swelling fellows would exclaim, sticking his arms akimbo and ruffling by the Southwesters, whom he regarded with great contempt, as men softened by mild climates and the luxurious fare of bread and bacon, and whom he stigmatized with the inglorious name of pork-eaters. The superiority assumed by these vainglorious swaggerers was, in general, tacitly accepted. Indeed, some of them had acquired great notoriety for deeds of hardihood and courage; for the fur-trade had its heroes, whose names resounded throughout the wilderness.

The influence and part played by the trapper and free trapper in the development of our great West has had up to this time but little consideration from either the government or the people. We have given entirely too much credit to "pathfinders" whose paths were as well known to the above as is the city street to the pedestrian. It is true, however, that they gave to the world a more complete description and placed these secret ways of the mountains in a more correct geographical position than the uneducated trapper was able to do.

There was not a stream or rivulet from the border of Mexico to the frozen regions of the North, but what was as familiar to these mountain rangers and lonesome wanderers, as the most traveled highway in our rural districts. The incentive was neither geographical knowledge nor the honor won by making new discoveries for the use and benefit of mankind in general, but a mercenary motive—the commercial value of the harmless and inoffensive little beaver. The trappers followed the course of the various streams looking for beaver signs and had no interest whatever in any other particular. Every stream had a certain gold value if it contained this industrious little animal, and so they followed them from their source to their mouth with this one object in view. For their own comfort and convenience they observed certain landmarks and the general topography of the country, in order that they might rove from one place to another with the least labor and inconvenience. In this manner they came to have a thorough and comprehensive knowledge of the geography and topography of the great West, and were in truth the only pathfinders; but they have been robbed even of this honor to a great extent.

The life of the solitary trapper in the mountains seems unendurable to one who is fond of social intercourse or of seeing now and then one of his fellow-beings. This habit of seclusion seemed to grow on some of the men and they really loved the life on that account, with all its hardships, privations, and dangers. The free trappers formed the aristocratic class of the fur-trade, and were the most interesting people in the mountains. They were bound to no fur company and were free to go where and when they pleased. It was the height of the ordinary trapper's ambition to attain such a position. They were men of bold and adventurous spirit, for none other would have had the courage to follow so dangerous an occupation. They were liable to have too much of this spirit of bravado, and frequently did extremely foolhardy things, nor could their leaders always control them in these excesses. They were exceedingly vain of their personal appearance and extravagantly fond of ornament for both themselves and their steeds, as well as their Indian wives. Indeed, they rivaled the proud Indian himself in the manner in which they bedecked themselves with these useless and cheap ornaments. They were utterly improvident, extremely fond of gambling and all games of chance, as well as all sorts of trials of skill, such as horsemanship and marksmanship; of course, the necessary wager to make it interesting was never wanting. As a general rule, the greater part of the proceeds of their labor was squandered at the first rendezvous or trading-post which they reached, and it was of great importance to the trader to be the first to reach such a rendezvous, thus securing the greater part of this most profitable trade.

Very little is known of their lonely vigils and wanderings, with a companion or two, in the defiles of the mountains, and of the dangers and privations they have had to endure. How frequently their bones have been left to bleach on the arid plains, as the result of Indian hatred and hostility, without the rites of burial—their names, unhonored and unsung, will never be known. Certain tribes were the uncompromising enemies of the trappers, and when they had the misfortune to meet, they waged a relentless war, until one or the entire party left the country or was exterminated. It is true, the returns were sometimes enormous, and had they exercised ordinary economy, even for one season, they could have retired from the dangers and privations of the mountains with a competence; but had they done so, it is altogether likely that they would sooner or later have again fallen victim to its allurements.

It is at the rendezvous and fort that the free trapper is seen in his true character. Here is usually spent the whole of his year's hard earnings in gambling, drinking, and finery. He wishes to establish the reputation of being a hale fellow, and he seldom fails so long as his money and credit last. Then he again returns to his lonely wanderings in the mountains, a sadder but not a wiser man, as the following year the same scene is enacted—provided he is so fortunate as to escape his treacherous enemies the Indians. The scenes presented at the mountain rendezvous in the early days must have been indeed wonderful, where hundreds of such characters were congregated; no pen, however clever, can do them full justice. The loss of life from other than natural causes from the years 1820 to 1840 cannot be estimated and will never be fully known. At each rendezvous, many former hale fellows were missing, never again to appear on this gay scene; their comrades recounted the manner of their death if known—their good traits were loyally lauded and their bad ones left untold—but the living did not take warning from these examples. Such was their life, hardships, dangers, and privations, also their pleasures—they lived only in the present, with little or no regard for the future. Irving gives the following extremely good description of them:

> The influx of this wandering trade has had its effects on
> the habits of the mountain tribes. They have found the
> trapping of the beaver their most profitable species of

hunting; and the traffic with the white man has opened to them sources of luxury of which they previously had no idea. The introduction of firearms has rendered them more successful hunters, but at the same time more formidable foes; some of them, incorrigibly savage and warlike in their nature, have found the expeditions of the fur traders grand objects of profitable adventure. To waylay and harass a band of trappers with their pack-horses when embarrassed in the rugged defiles of the mountains, has become as favorite an exploit with the Indians as the plunder of a caravan to the Arab of the desert. The Crows and Blackfeet, who were such terrors in the path of the early adventurers to Astoria, still continue their predatory habits, but seem to have brought them to greater system. They know the routes and resorts of the trappers; where to waylay them on their journeys; where to find them in the hunting seasons, and where to hover about them in winter-quarters.

The life of a trapper, therefore, is a perpetual state militant, and he must sleep with his weapons in his hands. A new order of trappers and traders, also, have grown out of this system of things. In the old times of the great North-west Company, when the trade in furs was pursued chiefly about the lakes and rivers, the expeditions were carried on in batteaux and canoes, The voyageurs or boatmen were the rank and file in the service of the trader, and even the hardy "men of the north," those great rufflers and game birds, were fain to be paddled from point to point of their migrations.

A totally different class has now sprung up—"the Mountaineers," the traders and trappers that scale the vast mountain chains, and pursue their hazardous vocations amidst their wild recesses. They move from place to place on horseback. The equestrian exercises, therefore, in which they are engaged, the nature of the countries they traverse, the vast plains and mountains, pure exhilarating in atmospheric qualities, seem to make them physically and mentally a more lively and mercurial race than the fur traders and trappers of former days, the self-vaunting "men of the north." A man who bestrides a horse, must be essentially different from a man who cowers in a canoe. We find them, accordingly, hardy, little, vigorous, and active; extravagant in word, and thought, and deed; heedless of hard-ship; daring of danger; prodigal of the present, and thoughtless of the future.

A difference is to be perceived even between these mountain hunters and those of the lower regions along the waters of the Missouri. The latter, generally French Creoles, live comfortably in cabins or log-huts, well sheltered from the inclemencies of the seasons. They are within the reach of frequent supplies from the settlements; their life is comparatively free from danger, and from most of the vicissitudes of the upper wilderness. The consequence is that they are less hardy, self-dependent and game-spirited than the mountaineer. If the latter by chance comes among them on his way to and from the settlements, he is like the game-cock among the common roosters of the poultry-yard. Accustomised to live in tents, or to bivouac in the open air, he despises the comforts and is impatient of the confinement of the log-house. If his meal is not ready in season, he takes his rifle, hies to the forest or prairie, shoots his own game, lights his fire, and cooks his repast. With his horse and his rifle, he is independent of the world, and spurns at all its restraints. The very superintendents at the lower posts will not put him to mess with the common men, the hirelings of the establishment, but treat him as something superior.

There is, perhaps, no class of men on the face of the earth, says Captain Bonneville, who lead a life of more continued exertion, peril, and excitement, and who are more enamored of their occupations, than the free trappers of the West. No toil, no danger, no privation can turn the trapper from his pursuit. His passionate excitement at times resembles a mania. In vain may the most vigilant and cruel savages beset his path; in vain may rocks, and precipices, and wintry torrents oppose his progress; let but a single track of a beaver meet his eye and he forgets all dangers and defies all difficulties. At times, he may be seen with his traps on his shoulder, buffeting his way across rapid streams, amidst floating blocks of ice; at other times, he is to be found with his traps swung on his back clambering the most rugged mountains, scaling or descending the most frightful precipices, searching, by routes inaccessible to the horse, and never before trodden

by white man, for springs and lakes unknown to his
comrades, and where he may meet with his favorite game.
Such is the mountaineer, the hardy trapper of the West;
and such, as we have slightly sketched it, is the wild Robin
Hood kind of life, with all its strange and motley populace,
now existing in full vigor among the Rocky Mountains.

Many of these men were in the mountains because of the
fascination of the exciting life, and were as loyally devoted
to it as any individual is to his vocation. Many who were
there, as well as many of the recruits, were men whose past
would not bear too close inspection. They frequently went to
the mountains to escape an outraged law, and remained not
because of their love for the wilderness, but through fear that
justice would be meted out to them should they return to the
States. This was always a dangerous and undesirable element.

Another class of recruits, and by far the most numerous,
was composed of young men or boys of an adventurous
disposition. The alluring stories of the mountains and the great
fortunes to be made in the trade, as illustrated by the very few
on whom dame fortune had smiled, were the inducements
held out to the inexperienced candidates for the mountains.
The failures were, however, not mentioned and the trials,
hard-ships, dangers, and loss of life were scarcely taken into
consideration. A great majority of these young men soon
learned from that wonderful teacher—experience—that
it was as difficult to accumulate fortunes in the mountains
as elsewhere, and infinitely more dangerous. Such was the
school of hardship and privation from which many good men
graduated and later became settlers and men of prominence in
the rapidly developing great West.

Many of these men, particularly those in the employ of the
British companies and not only the trappers but the officers of
the company as well, contracted marriages with Indian women
and for this reason did not wish to return to civilization and
their former homes. They therefore remained in the West and
their families developed with the rapid growth of this new
country, and in this manner some of the leading families have a
trace of aboriginal blood in their veins, of which they are justly
proud.

Such was the school which graduated the scout and guide of later days. It was they who conducted the scientific expeditions sent out by the government, the surveying as well as exploring parties; it was they who guided the first emigrants by the overland routes to Oregon and California; and they who ferreted out in their peregrinations in the mountains the passage-ways, for none of the above expeditions would have ventured into this *terra incognita* without one of these old trappers as guide. Even the army, while in pursuit of hostile Indians, had its corps of experienced scouts and guides, which was largely made up of these mountain-men. For this kind of service they were well fitted, as they were inured to hard-ships and dangers. The decline of the fur-trade practically left them stranded, and in looking about for employment they were glad to accept such positions; nevertheless, their services have never been properly appreciated.

First among the challenges facing the mountain man was the problem of getting himself—his expedition or enterprise—west to the mountains, where the valuable fur-bearing animals were most plentiful.

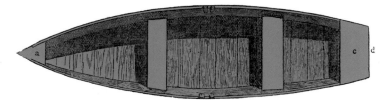

BATEAU

The *bateau,* from the French word for "boat," was most often a flat-bottomed, keel-less affair, framed in oak or other hardwood, sided in sawed pine planks and caulked with a pine-tar pitch or other tree resin. These ordinary boats—sometimes called *jon-boats*—were, to mix a metaphor, the workhorses of America's inland waterways, and might be as much as fifty or sixty feet long. They were either double-bowed, if ease of maneuver was the imperative, or single bowed with a square stern, when the aim was to maximize the amount of cargo to be carried. Though highly stable afloat, their bulk made them difficult to portage, which tended to limit their use to larger watercourses. Very often, they were fitted with a simple box device that allowed for the steeping of a (usually) stumpy mast.

KEELBOAT

The *keelboat* of this era was a long, narrow, keel-built vessel, often with a cabin or other shelter, usually located amidships. Propelled either by an arrangement of sweeps or by poling depending on the plan of decking, they often sported a mast and boom apparatus well forward, and were steered by rudder or oar. Frequently, the keelboat was the largest and most substantial craft in the flotilla, and often served as headquarters for the commercial or military expedition.

WHALEBOAT

Originally a sea-going vessel much in use in the whale
fisheries and the Atlantic coastal trade, the *whaleboat* was soon
adapted for transport on the inland waterways of the Americas.
Double-bowed.

PIROGUE

Essentially a large, open boat, often double-bowed and flat-bottomed, they could be rowed or sailed.

In the era of the mountain men, a *pirogue* tended to be of considerable size, and heavy enough to withstand the discharge of swivel guns mounted in their bows.

FLATBOAT

The fur companies felt as great an urgency to get supplies west to the trading posts as they did to remove furs east to market. The *flatboat* was a relatively inexpensive and common answer to this need to move goods in bulk.

The lumber for these rectangular, flat-bottomed scows ordinarily came from cottonwoods, hardwoods, and pines. They were purpose-built, usually constructed for a particular shipment; and were expendable, in that they were often wholly modified at their journey's end, or scrapped altogether and sold off for the value of their planking.

DUGOUT CANOE

Also called a *log canoe*, the dugout is strong, serviceable, and durable. Its construction is simple and it may be made quite light. This canoe may be made of pine, butternut, black-ash basswood, or cotton-wood. The best are hewn from pine. A log suitable for this should be large, sound and free of knots.

First it should be cut on two opposite sides of the log to a size corresponding to the depth of the intended vessel. On one side the cutting should not be in a straight line, but should run out at the surface of the log in order to give enough of a rise at the bow and stern. This is sometimes performed before the log is even cut or the tree is felled. Once the log is on the ground it is laid with that side uppermost which is to form the gunwale.

Next the outlines of the sides are marked with a line and chalk or a burnt stick. The general rule for laying out a canoe is to measure it into three equal sections; the two end sections are for the bow and stern. For a large canoe, the bow should be shaped somewhat more sharply than the stern. Likewise, the width of the vessel at the point where the curves of the bow start—below the gunwale—should be a little greater than at any other point. This difference can be easily managed when finishing off the sides, after the general shape is attained. If the canoe is very large it may be a good idea to attend to this task in the first hewing. The object in giving the dugout canoe a greater width here is to promote an ease of motion in the water. The same principle that governs in the construction of a larger vessel—and is seen in the shape of the duck or goose—applies to the shaping of a larger canoe.

A small log canoe, intended to carry no more than two persons, may be carved with the same sharpness at both ends, and needs no variation in its width. It may be run either end foremost. A canoe made in this way, if narrow and very sharp, is easily one of the swiftest and most useful of the mountain man's boats.

Both ends of a well-made canoe are curved upward from the middle of the gunwale, and the stern rises a little from the line of the bottom. When the tree is sound, a canoe may be worked very thin and thus be light and easily carried.

Keeping all of these points in mind, the canoe is hewn to something resembling its final outer shape; then the inside is dug out with axes and adze; finally it is neatly and smoothly finished—on the outside with ax and draw-shave, and on the inside with round edged adze.

BUILDING A BIRCH-BARK CANOE

Though not as durable as the dugout, nor as easily constructed, the great advantage of a bark canoe is its lightness. It is the vessel of choice on waterways where portaging is necessary. The canoe may be of any length. One of fifteen or twenty feet can easily be carried on the shoulders of two men; while a smaller one, ten or twelve feet long, is managed by one man without much difficulty.

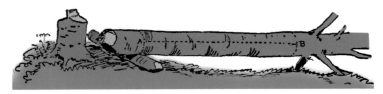

The bark can be harvested in one of two ways; either by felling a tree onto a skid—this permits you to strip it easily and makes real sense if you intend to use the wood of the tree in your construction—or you can strip it from a standing tree.

The birch tree is selected for straightness, smoothness, freedom from knots or limbs, toughness of bark, and for size—though this is not so important—as you will likely need to piece out the sides.

Bark can be peeled when the sap is flowing or when the tree is not frozen, at any time in late spring, summer, and early fall—called summer bark—or in winter during a thaw, when the tree is not frozen and when the sap has begun to flow. Summer bark peels readily, is smooth inside, and of a yellow color, which turns reddish upon exposure to the sun. Winter bark adheres closely to the tree and often brings up part of the inner bark, which on exposure turns dark red. This rough surface ought to be moistened and scraped away.

Torch

After the bark has been peeled, the inside surface can be warmed with a torch, which softens and makes it supple. This torch may be made of a bundle of birch bark held in a split stick.

The bark is then rolled up like a carpet, with inside surface out, tightly bound and carried to your worksite. Lay it where the sunshine will not harden it. The first effect of heat is to make it pliant, but long exposure to heat or to dry atmosphere makes it hard and brittle.

The gunwales of the canoe are composed of four lengths of cedar wood, about a quarter inch thick by an inch or more in width—two for each side—one to go on the inside edge and on the outside. The width and shape of vessel is determined by the length of the cross-pieces used in separating the sides of the gunwale frame.

Lay the bark on flat ground with the weathered side up. Weigh the center down with several good-sized round stones. The part which forms the bottom of the canoe should be one whole piece. If it is not large enough, pieces are sewn onto it.

Measure out the length of the canoe and, at each end close together, drive two stakes firmly into the ground. The bark is then folded on the middle line, with inside of the bark outward, and inserted between the two stakes. The ends of the bark should extend beyond the stakes far enough to facilitate the fashioning of curved bows at each end of the canoe.

On each side drive several stakes into the ground closely corresponding to the shape of the gunwale frame and lay it atop the stakes. This will allow the edges of the bark to be brought up, folded over, and fastened with a winding stitch to the frame.

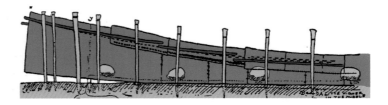

Now lash the ends of the gunwale frames together and adjust and lash the cross-pieces to the gunwale. This will largely determine the overall shape of the canoe.

Mark out the contour of the bows and cut the bark into that shape, stitch the pieces together, cover the edge with a folded strip of bark, and stitch again. Stiffen the bow by bending and

32

wedging a three-foot long, one inch by one quarter inch, cedar lath inside the bow(s). Lash to the underside of the gunwale ends and seat it with resin or pitch.

Remove the stone weights and stiffen the bark by lining the inside with long, thin strips of cedar. They should be placed longitudinally, lap where their ends meet, and be seated with pine pitch or resin.

The knees or ribs are made of strips of ash or any wood that is firm and elastic, and should be about one quarter inch thick by two or more inches. They ride perpendicularly to the cedar lining, are bent down to the bottom, and lashed to the gunwale frame. They should be placed close together the whole length of the canoe.

Smear the inside and all the seams with pine pitch or resin.

BULL BOAT

One method of ferrying streams is by means of what the mountaineers call a *bull boat*, the frame-work of which is made of willows bent into the shape of a short and wide skiff, with a flat bottom.

Building a Bull Boat

Willows grow upon the banks of many streams and can be bent into the desired shape. To make a boat with one hide, a number of straight willows are cut about an inch in diameter, the ends sharpened and driven into the ground, forming a framework in the shape of a half egg-shell cut through the longitudinal axis. Where these rods cross they are firmly tied. A stout rod is then heated and bent around the frame in such a position that the edges of the hide, when laid over it and drawn tight, will just reach it. This rod forms the gunwale, which is tied to the ribs. Small rods are then wattled in so as to make

it symmetrical and strong, after which the green or soaked hide is pulled over the edges, sewed to the gunwales, and left to dry. The rods are then cut off even with the gunwale, and the boat is ready for use.

To build a boat with two or more hides: a stout pole of the desired length is placed upon the ground for a keel, the ends turned up and secured by a lariat; willow rods of the required dimensions are then cut, heated, and bent into the proper shape for knees, after which their centers are placed at equal distances upon the keel and firmly tied with cords. The knees are retained in their proper curvature by cords around the ends. After a sufficient number of them have been placed upon the keel, two poles of suitable dimensions are heated, bent around the ends for a gunwale, and firmly lashed to each knee. Smaller willows are then interwoven, so as to model the frame.

Green or soaked hides are cut into the proper shape to fit the frame and sewed together with buckskin strings. Then the frame of the boat is placed in the middle, the hide drawn up snug around the sides, and secured with raw-hide thongs to the gunwale. The boat is then turned bottom upward and left to dry, after which the seams where they have been sewn are covered with a mixture of melted tallow, pitch, or resin. The craft is now ready for launching.

A boat of this kind is very light and serviceable, but after a time becomes water-logged, and should always be turned bottom upward to dry whenever it is not in the water. Two men can easily build a *bull boat* of three hides in two days. This will easily carry ten men.

A TRAPPER'S RAFT

When no canoe or other vessel was at hand, the trapper's common resort was to the two or three log raft.

Not only as a way getting of him across a river or creek, reasonably dry-shod, but also a means and tool for tending his traps up and down the particular waterway.

It was easily constructed and as a working platform it was preferable to a canoe.

HORSE AND MULE
PACKING

"Packing is an art as old as the first time a man moved, and had
an animal to help him do it."

—Norman Maclean

The outfit needed for packing camp equipment is, for each
horse or mule, a pack-saddle, woolen blankets, pack cinch, 35
or 40 feet of manila rope, another rope of the same size, 20
feet long, a pair of *alforjas*, a pair of hobbles, and a bell to put
on the horse when it is turned out for the night.

A pack-saddle consists of two crosses of hardwood, fastened
to two flat, round-end pieces of wood, and to this is attached
breeching, breast straps and usually two cinches, and other
necessary strap work.

A good pack-saddle is strong and well made, of good
materials. The leather is a peculiar kind that will not tighten
when tied into knots, for the cinch adjustments are usually tied
instead of fastened with buckles. When selecting a pack-saddle,

be sure that the breeching and breast straps are long enough for any horse on which the saddle may be used.

Be certain also that the saddle fits the horse reasonably well, or it will cause more trouble. Most of the pack-horses used in the mountains are more or less hollow backed, and the saddle base should not be too long or it will rest on the ends only. On the other hand, if too short it will not be so stable and will also hurt the horse. The double cinch saddle, such as shown in the illustration, is by far the best.

Alforjas are sacks that hang on the sides of the saddle, in which are placed all of the small articles of the outfit. They are made of very heavy duck, leather bound, and have straps or loops of rope with which to suspend them from the saddle forks. The proper size is about 24 inches wide, 18 inches high and, when opened out, 9 inches deep. When packing an outfit, the horse should be tied and the blanket should be folded and placed on the horse's back. It should not be less than four folds thick and should extend a little ahead and a little behind the saddle base. It must also come down far enough on the sides to form a pad for the *alforjas* or panniers to keep them from rubbing and chafing the animal.

The saddle should then be placed on the folded blanket. Now, at this point, if you want to be kind to the poor horse, grasp the blanket between the two pieces of the saddle base and pull it up a little, so that it is loose over the horse's back. This will allow the saddle to settle down under the weight of the pack and not bind, which it is sure to do if the blanket is not loosened a little as advised. Then both cinches should be tightened and the breeching and breast straps properly adjusted.

The panniers are then filled with the small articles of the camp equipment and hung on the forks of the saddle. If the packer is at all conscientious, as he should be, he will see that each sack is of the same weight and that there are no hard or sharp objects so placed that they will injure the animal. Articles which are too big to go into the sacks are then placed on top, where they will rest firmly and not hurt the horse, and the blankets and tent are folded and spread over the top of saddle and panniers.

At this stage commences what is generally considered the trick of packing: tying the pack to the horse. There are many forms of pack hitch in use and any of them may be learned quite easily by an observing person, nevertheless tying a pack properly can scarcely be done at the first attempt. The most popular of pack ties is what is known as the diamond hitch and, all things considered, is probably the best on the list.

To throw the diamond hitch, proceed as follows: having tied one end of the long rope to the ring of the pack cinch, go to the near side (left) of the horse and throw the cinch over the pack and horse, then reach under the horse and pick up the cinch. The hooked end of the cinch is now toward you. Draw back on the rope until you have all of the slack and pull the rope down on the near side to the hook of the cinch; double it here and give it a twist, as shown in Fig. 1, then hook the loop to the cinch. Now double the free portion of the rope and shove it through under the part marked by the arrow, from the back, forming loop A, as shown in Fig. 2. Now give this loop a twist as shown in Fig. 3, to bring the free portion of the rope down farther towards the near side. Next grasp this rope at the place marked by the arrow in Fig. 3, and draw up a part of the free rope forming loop B, as shown in Fig. 4.

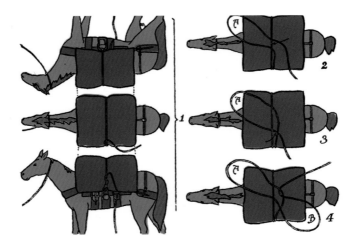

All of this time you have been keeping the rope that crosses the pack fairly tight. You now go to the off side and pull loop A down over and under the pack, then come back and put loop B under the pack on the near side. This will leave the hitch as in Fig. 5 and it is ready for tightening. Start first by pulling the rope at A, then at B, C, D, E, F, G, and H, successively. The end of the rope H is then tied to the ring in the pack cinch at the off side, and the diamond hitch is completed. The ropes should all be quite tight, and if they grow loose after awhile they should be tightened again.

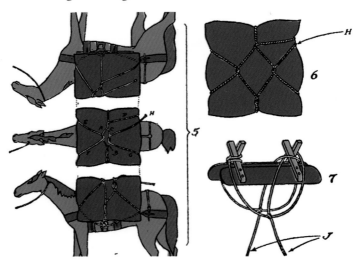

There is another very simple way of tying a diamond hitch, which though not quite like the one described in detail, is the same in principle. It is shown very plainly in the three diagrams reproduced here. As in the first method the rope and cinch are thrown across the pack to the off side and the cinch is picked up from beneath the horse, then the rope is drawn up and hooked to the cinch, but the little twist is not put in the rope as in the first method. The free portion of the rope is then thrown across the pack to the off side so that it is parallel with and behind the first rope. Then double this rope on the top of the pack and push it under the first rope from the rear, as shown in Fig. 8. Now bring this loop back over and push it through again, as in Fig. 9, forming the small loop A. Now take the free end of the rope down under the pack on the near side, back and up at the rear, through the loop A again. This is illustrated in Fig. 10. The free end of the rope then goes down under the pack from the rear on the off side and fastens to the cinch ring. The rope is tightened the same as in the other method. This hitch is as good as the other and is more easily remembered, although not as easily tied as the one first described.

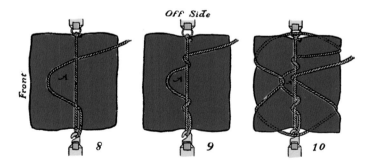

Either of these pack ties may be managed easily by one man, but they are tied more rapidly by two men, one standing on the off side and the other on the near side, so that neither need walk around the horse. Then there is the additional advantage in that the rope may be drawn up tight and there is no danger that it will slip, as one or the other of the men can be holding the rope all the time the pack is being tied.

In addition to the pack ties described, there is another hitch that should be learned, as it is useful for securing packages to the pack saddle when *alforjas* are not used (also for holding packs to the sides of the saddle while tying the diamond hitch). There are several methods of fixing a sling rope and the mode I am going to describe is illustrated in Fig. 7.

For this purpose the shorter length of rope is used. It is doubled in the middle and looped around the front forks of the pack saddle, then one-half of the rope is taken to the near side and the other is dropped on the off side. Taking either half of the rope, you allow sufficient slack to hold the pack at the proper height then bring the rope around the rear forks, then down to the center of the slack portion, where it is tied. The pack is then fixed in this loop and the other side is arranged the same way. After both packs are properly slung, the ends of the rope are brought up on top and tied together.

There are many forms of pack hitches other than those described, although the diamond hitch is most used and more popular than any of the others.

A pack-horse should never be overloaded, and the animal cannot carry as great a load as many people expect. Two hundred pounds is the limit for any pack, and one hundred and fifty pounds is a more reasonable load. For long journeys the pack, per horse or mule, should not weigh this much. A hundred or one hundred and twenty-five pounds is all that should be allotted to any animal.

A pack train may consist of any number of pack animals, and if there are enough riders in the party, one man rides between each two pack-horses. By that I mean one rider goes ahead, leading a horse behind him. That horse is followed by another rider, then another pack-horse, etc. If there are not enough men in the party for this, two pack animals are placed between two riders. The men may lead the horses if they are inclined to wander from the route, but ordinarily this is not necessary, as the animals will keep in line. But if you lead a pack-horse, do not grow tired of holding the rope and tie it to the horn of the saddle. This is a dangerous practice and may result in serious injury to the one who is so thoughtless, for the pack horse may become frightened and bolt or may swing around, wrapping the rope around the rider.

Pack animals are always more or less troublesome, and the man who uses them should have a bountiful supply of patience. At night the animals are hobbled, which means that their front feet are fastened together with hobbles, so that they cannot travel fast or far. Too much dependence should not be placed on these retarders, for Western horses soon learn to travel quite rapidly when thus impeded, and will sometimes set out for home while the master sleeps. A good practice is to picket one or two horses in the best spots of pasture to be found, and hobble the remaining animals. They are not so likely to leave if this is done, and if they do, the picketed horses must remain behind, which insures at least a mount with which to follow the runaways. Also put a bell on each horse, as this will aid in locating the animals in the morning.

On the trail, western mules and horses rarely get any food except what they can find at night or while they are not in use, and on the plains or in the mountains where vegetation is scanty they sometimes do not get as much as they require. Under such circumstances they should not be loaded too heavily or traveled too far in a day, and it may even be necessary, on a long journey to take an occasional day of rest to allow them to recuperate.

CROSSING A RIVER
OR STREAM

It's an old and well-established custom among mountain men to always cross the stream where they intend to encamp for the night, This rule should never be broken if the stream or river is to be forded, as a rise during the night might well detain the party for several days in awaiting the fall of the waters.

A party traveling with a pack train and arriving on the banks of a deep stream will not always have the time to stop or the means to construct a boat. Should their luggage be such as to become damaged by wetting, the best plan is to untie and remove the pack from the animal and wrap it securely in heavy canvas or a green beef or buffalo hide. Spread the wrapping on the ground and place the articles in the center. Then bring the sides up so as to completely envelope the package, securing the whole with rope or rawhide. Place it in the water with a rope attached to one end and tow it across. The mountain man was always careful to keep the materials used for this kind of wrapping dry and well greased.

If a mounted party with pack animals arrive on the borders of a rapid stream too deep to ford and where the banks are high and abrupt with perhaps only one place where the animals can get out on the opposite shore, it would not be safe to drive or ride them in. Some of them may be carried by the swift current too far downstream, and thereby endanger not only their own lives, but the lives of their riders as well. A simple and safe method for getting your pack-train across such a river or stream is have two or three of the best swimmers in your party make their way across carrying one end of a sturdy rope, while the rest of the party who have remained on the bank make their end of the line fast around the neck of the best-swimming horse or mule. Next all the other animals are secured in this fashion, one to another with better swimmers foremost. After the whole pack train has been strung out in this single line, the first horse or mule is led carefully into the water, while the men on the opposite bank, pulling on the rope, and direct him across, aiding him in stemming the current. As soon as this first animal strikes bottom, he pulls on those behind him, thereby assisting them in making their landings as well. Where rivers are wide and the current swift, they should always, if possible, be forded obliquely downstream, as the action of the water against the string of animals is a great help in carrying them across.

During seasons of high water, mountain men often encountered rivers that rose well above a fording stage, and remained in that condition for many days. If the hunter or trapper was alone, his only choice was to swim his horse; but if he retained the seat on his saddle, his weight pressed the animal down into the water, and cramped its movements considerably. The better plan was to tie a line to the bridle-bit, then drive the horse or mule into the stream and holding the animal by the tail, allow it to tow him across. Should the animal turn from its course or attempt to turn back, he could be checked with the line. If the rider chose to remain in the saddle he was careful to allow his mount a loose rein, never pulling on it except to guide. If he needed to steady himself, he could always grab the mane.

TRAVOIS

The basic *travois* is of Native American origin. It is essentially an A-frame construction and consists of two long wooden staffs (often tepee poles) lashed together at the narrower ends, and braced by lashing one or two cross-pieces mid-way to the open end.

The width of the travois was determined by the length and placement of these bracing cross-pieces. This bracing also served as a rudimentary platform upon which the load could be tied.

A travois might be pulled (depending on its size) either by dog or horse—or even by a man or woman—and was particularly useful in getting loads across broken ground.

SNOWSHOES

The first thing is to plan the size, shape and general character of the shoes. Making the frames, or bows, are the first steps.

The tree from which the frames are to be made should be not more than eight inches in diameter, and one of six inches is better. It should have drooping branches, and ought to have eight or ten feet of the trunk straight and clean, free of limbs, and absolutely without a twist to the grain.

After the tree has been felled and a section of the proper length cut off, a groove about one and a half inches deep is carefully cut the entire length along one side. Take care not to strike hard, as that might injure the wood.

When the groove is finished a similar one is cut on the opposite side. The stick should be split with wooden wedges, and if it is properly done the split will follow the grooves. The best half should then be chosen for the proposed snowshoe frames, and this should be ripped lengthwise with a saw, or split, as desired. Each of the pieces will make a frame or bow.

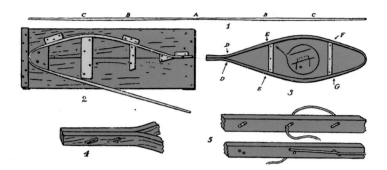

One side of the stick is then cut and planed until it is perfectly straight—its face at a right angle to the bark side. There should be nothing taken off the bark side, not even the bark, until after the wood is bent into shape for the snowshoe frame.

Next the third side of the stick is marked off with a marking gauge and either cut or sawed to the mark. The fourth side, the inside of the stick, which will be the inside of the finished frame, is then cut down to the proper dimensions, but on this side an even thickness is not maintained, the toe portion being cut thinnest, with the heel—ends of the stick—coming next.

For a snowshoe of average size, say 44 inches in length and 14 inches wide, the stick should measure eight and a half feet in length, one inch in width, seven-eighths inch thick at the parts which will become the middle of the shoe (B to C in figure one), one-half inch at A, and about five-eighths inch at the ends.

Before anything more can be done with the wood a form for bending the frames must be made. A convenient form is shown in figure two. For steaming the wood properly it is necessary to have a steaming box, which is merely a long case made of narrow boards, open at both ends. The stick is placed in this case and the steam from a boiling tea kettle turned in one end so that the hot steam travels the entire length. The wood should be steamed for an hour and then it is ready for bending.

Figure two shows how the wood is bent and secured on the form. The toe must be formed very carefully, bending only a little at first, then releasing, then bending a little more, and so on until the wood can be easily and safely bent to complete shape and secured by nailing blocks to the form. The wood should be allowed to dry thoroughly on the form before filling, and this will require at least two weeks.

After the frames are dry they may be taken from the form, the tail end of each fastened and the crossbars fitted into place. The ends may be secured with a wood screw until after the frames have been strung, but the screw should then be removed and the ends tied with rawhide, through gimlet holes, the part between being counter sunk so that the thongs will be protected from wear. This is shown in figure four.

The crossbars are pieces of flat, strong wood, about one and a fourth inches wide and nearly a half-inch thick, with rounded edges. These should be placed about 16 or 17 inches apart, measuring from center to center, and so placed that when the frame is suspended on the hands midway between these two sticks the tail will outweigh the toe by just a few ounces. These cross-bars should be carefully mortised into the frame as shown in the small diagram in center of figure three.

In both sides of the frame from D to E, also from F to G, gimlet holes are bored through the bows from outside to inside at intervals of two inches, or a little more, the holes being in pairs obliquely placed, and countersunk between. Three holes are also bored through each crossbar, as shown.

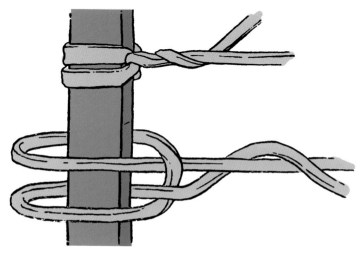

The frames are now ready for filling. Regarding material for filling, for ordinary use, there is nothing equal to cowhide, a fairly heavy skin. A whole hide will fill several pairs of shoes. The portion along the back is best and this should be used for filling the middle section. The lighter parts from the edges of the skin will do for stringing the heels and toes. All strands should be cut length-wise of the skin, and full length—their width depending on the thickness of the skin. It is well to cut several trial widths, so that the proper weight of strand may be determined. For a coarse webbed shoe, the thongs, after being stretched and dried, should be about five-sixteenths of an inch wide for the middle portion of the shoe; for the ends an eighth inch is sufficiently heavy. These strands of hide should all be soaked and stretched thoroughly, allowed to dry while stretched, and then soaked again just before using, and strung into the frames while wet.

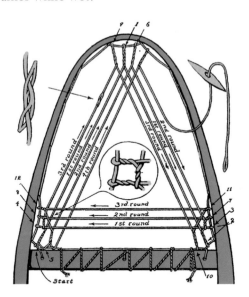

The ends are filled first. A strand of the water-soaked rawhide is stretched tightly around the inside of the toe portion through the little gimlet holes, as shown in figure five, starting and finishing at one of the holes in the forward crossbar. This thong is called the lanyard, and its purpose is to hold the filling, which is woven into the toe.

50

A small needle of very hard wood, or bone, is used for filling the ends. Starting in the lower left-hand corner it goes up to the part marked 1, passes around the lanyard, twists back around itself about an inch and then goes down to 2, there passing around the lanyard and again twisting around itself, then around the lanyard at 3, a single twist, and then across to 4, where it again turns around the lanyard, then twists down around the first strand to the starting point, under the lanyard at 5 and up to 6. From there the strand loops and twists the same as in the first round, except that at the lower corners it loops back around the first round, then twists around itself, then around the lanyard, and on the same as before. This looping back of every second round is continued until the filling extends across the entire forward part of the toe, when it is discontinued, and each round is made like the first. This looping back throws the filling alternately from side to side. The filling must be stretched in very tightly and must not be allowed to slip. When one strand is used up another is joined on in the manner shown. See that every round crosses the others in the proper way, and all the twists are made alike. The weave will finish at the center of the crossbar.

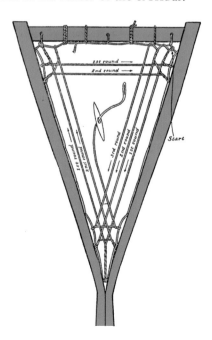

The filling in the tail end or heel starts at the upper right-hand corner and finishes in the middle of the crossbar. Great care should be used to get the twists and loops right, and to see that the thongs cross in the proper way.

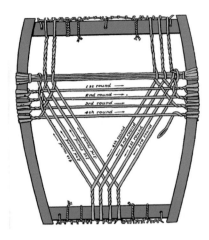

Filling the middle section is simpler than it appears at first glance—it is practically a repetition of the system used in the toe portion. The edges of the wood should be rounded slightly to prevent them cutting the thongs.

While the system of stringing this part may appear quite intricate, it is in reality simple, and is the more elaborate arrangement of the forward portion that makes this section appear so complicated. The stout bunch of thongs shown in the drawing, known as the toe cord, are strung in first, the rawhide strand being tightly stretched and crossing the frame some four or five times, a loop being thrown around the whole on the inside of the frame on both sides in the last round. This should be executed so that the last loop will be on the right-hand side. The thong then loops around this bunch of cords again about an inch from the frame, from there being strung up around the cross-bar, and then twisting around itself back to the starting point. From there it passes down diagonally to the center of the rear cross-bar, where it loops and twists again, then up to the upper left-hand corner where it twists up the same as on the opposite side. From here it will be noted that the thong runs down a short distance and loops around the left side of the frame. The simple loop used for this purpose is clearly shown in the small drawing. From this loop, the rawhide strand twists back about an inch, then runs straight across the shoe to the right, where the loop is repeated. This completes the first round of the filling. The second round starts in about the same way as the first, going up to the crossbar at the left of the first round, twisting back to the toe cord, from there to the rear crossbar, then up to the left-hand corner. Here the system changes, for the strand is run up and twisted around the toe cord and first round of filling before it is looped to the frame. After looping, it is brought across to the right, where it again loops and twists, and then twists around the toe cord and first round of filling exactly as on the left, after which it is run down to the rear crossbar. In this way the stringing continues, every second round twisting forward around the preceding two. This binds the filling firmly and, it should be noted, also alternates the successive rounds from side to side. When the process of filling has progressed so far that there are four twists around the forward crossbar on each side, this twisting should be stopped and the remainder of the forward portion left open, for this is where the foot of the wearer works through when walking. This open space should measure about four and a half inches in width, and if it does not, the filling must be shifted. In very coarse meshed shoes three twists on each side will be all that can be given. An extra turn around the toe cord should also be made on each of these two twists of the filling, for considerable strain is put onto this portion. From this point on, instead of running forward and twisting around the crossbar, the filling simply twists around the toe cord. Be careful to keep the filling smooth and the toe cord flat, otherwise sore feet will result from wearing the shoes. The weave finishes in the center of the toe cord and there the end of the thong should be securely and neatly fastened. The last touch is to wind a strand of rawhide about the twisted thongs on each side of the foot opening and around the toe cord, to make these parts smooth and protect them from wear.

In the drawings of the heel and toe sections it will be noted that I have shown the web tied to the crossbars with twine. This is not a permanent feature, for when the center of the shoe has been filled these strings may be removed.

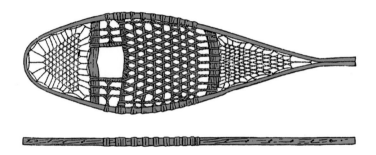

Snowshoes require care, not only while in use, but at other times as well, as they are strung with rawhide; a material very susceptible to heat and moisture. If the shoes are not dried thoroughly after becoming wet, the stringing will rot, while if dried too rapidly the filling becomes brittle and breaks when put to a strain. In camp snowshoes are suspended from the ceiling by a wire, because mice will eat the filling if they can reach them. Shoes should be watched closely for worn strands and when a string looks dangerously weak the shoe should be repaired at once.

I used frequently to lose Fred.

Diversion on a Mountain Trail.

AN INDIAN TOBOGGAN

For winter travel over deep snows there is no better sled in the world than the Indian toboggan. For the trapper during winter it was often indispensable, and without it the native hunters of the North would find great difficulty in getting their furs to market. All through the winter season the various trading posts were visited by the trappers, many of whom had traveled hundreds of miles on their snowshoes with their heavily laden toboggans. Arriving at their market, they sold or traded their stock of furs, and likewise disposed of their toboggans, reserving only their snowshoes to aid them in their long tramp homewards.

Building an Indian Toboggan

The first need is a board about eight feet in length and sixteen or more inches in width. Oak is the best wood for the purpose, although hickory, basswood, or ash will do excellently. It should be planed or sawed to a thickness of about a third of an inch and should be free of knots. If a single board of the required width is not easily found, two boards may be used, and secured side by side by three cleats, one at each end and the other in the middle. A single board is much preferred, if it can be had.

Next, seven or eight wooden cross pieces of a length equivalent to the width of the board are needed. Four old broomsticks, cut in the required lengths, will do the trick perfectly, and if these are not available, other sticks of similar dimensions should be used. The two side pieces are needed next. These should be about five feet in length, and of a thickness exactly similar to the cross pieces.

Next, procure a few pairs of leather shoestrings or some strips of tough calfskin. With these collected we now begin the work of putting the parts together.

Begin by laying the cross pieces at equal distances along the board; across these and near their ends, lay the two side pieces, as seen in the illustration.

Using a drill, bore four holes through the board, beneath the end of each cross piece, and also directly under the side piece. It's a good idea to mark the various points for the holes with a pencil, after which the sticks can be removed and the work much more easily performed. The four holes should be about an inch apart, or so disposed as to mark the four corners of a square inch.

It is also necessary to make other holes along the length of the cross pieces, as seen in the illustration.

The line on these can also be marked with the pencil across the board and the holes made afterwards. These should also be an inch apart, and only two in number at each point; one on each side of the stick. When all the holes are completed, turn the board over in order to complete preparations on the other side.

The object of these various holes is for the passage of the leather shoe-strings we will use to secure the cross pieces firmly to the board.

In order to prevent these loops from wearing off on the underside, make small grooves on the underside connecting the holes. This allows the leather string to sink into the wood, where it will be protected from injury. A narrow chisel is the best tool for this purpose. When the underside is finished the board may be turned over and the cross pieces and sides again arranged in place as described above.

Secure the pieces to the board by the leather strings through the various holes, always knotting on the upper surface and taking care that the knots are firmly tied. The ends of all the cross pieces will require a double cross stitch through the four holes beneath, in order to secure the side pieces as well. This is plainly shown in the small diagram (*a*). The front end of each side piece underneath should now be sharpened to a point to allow for the bend at the front of the toboggan.

The cross piece at the front end should be secured to the *underside of the board*, so that as it bends over it will appear on the upper edge, as in the illustration. The board should then be bent with a graceful curve, and thus held in position by a rope or strip of leather at each extremity of the end cross piece and attached to the ends of the third cross piece.

If the bending is difficult and there is danger of breaking the board, an application of boiling water will render it pliable.

The draw-strings are finally attached to the ends of the second cross piece, and the toboggan is complete.

It may now be laden with two or three hundred pounds of merchandize and will be found to draw over the surface of the snow with perfect ease. For coasting over the crust there is nothing like it.

FORTS AND TRADING POSTS

Once the trappers and traders were able to get their expedition West to beaver country, their immediate task was to offload their gear from the myriad of boats in their flotilla—all the supplies, tools, trade-goods, and other impedimenta—and to establish a trading post or base camp from which to operate. The trading post was much more than a sort of general store in the middle of the woods. It also served as the enterprise's headquarters in the field, as blacksmith and carpenter's shop, stock yard, warehouse, and sometimes as a military post.

The location or site of the post was of critical importance; the choice of which often spelled success or failure for the venture. The trick was to get as far West, well enough into beaver country, for it to function both as a point of transshipment—trade goods in, furs out—as well as a hub or center from which the company trappers worked, and to which the independents and native peoples could bring their pelts to trade.

The first consideration was to find a spot on high, well-drained ground, close enough to a river or other good sized waterway so as to permit reasonable access to transport to and from the post, but set far enough back from the bank so that it was not washed away by every spring flood.

Since the post was nearly always constructed of wood, there needed to be a good supply of timber at hand. A secondary source of fresh water—a nearby creek or spring—was a big advantage.

Defensibility was also an important consideration in citing and building a post. A stout *blockhouse*, *stockade*, and *a clear field of fire* were three elements upon which the physical security of the post or fort most depended.

STOCKADE BUILDING

First stake out the perimeter of the stockade. Nearly all forts were constructed as rectangles.

Dig a three-foot deep trench—the width of which will depend on the diameter of the log you intend to use—along the lines of this perimeter.

Cut a sufficient number of straight logs of a uniform diameter and length, remembering that, owing to the depth of the trench, a thirteen-foot log will result in a ten-foot high wall. Very often the logs are split, thus halving, roughly, the number of trees that need to be felled and dragged to the site.

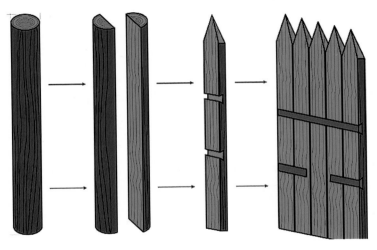

Seat the logs upright in the trench and winch them one to the other as snuggly as possible, holding them together with long cross pieces or batons. Often whole sections of wall were laid out on the ground, braced together, and then muscled up and into the trench.

Back fill the trench with large stones and the excavated gravel, and you have the rudiments of a stockade fort.

LEAN-TO, TENTS, AND TEPEES

Lean-tos were in general use among the old veteran trappers of all countries, and there is a certain charm in a shelter so quickly constructed from the rude materials of the woods, which portable tents do not possess. Drive two sets of forked sticks into the ground. Lay cross-pieces into the two sets of forks. Roof it by lying smaller sticks across the cross-pieces, and also vertically to form a back wall.

Tents are of several kinds. Those most commonly used by the mountain man were the house-tent, fly-tent, shanty-tent, and half-tent (or shelter-tent).

The *house-tent* is made of two prop-poles and a ridge-pole. It is generally closed on one end and buttoned up at the other. The sides are perpendicular for two or three feet before the slope commences, and the stay-ropes are fastened to the eaves.

The *fly-tent* is generally a large, square piece of canvas, with ropes extending from opposite sides. This is thrown over a ridge-pole or over a rope extending between two trees. The sides are held to the proper slope by tightening and pegging the side ropes to the ground. Fly-tents are also made with ends, which can be lowered, and the whole tent may be pegged close to the ground.

The *shanty-tent* consists of two sets of prop-poles with cross-pieces, one set of prop-poles being roughly twice the height of the other, but conforming to the cut of the canvas.

The *shelter-tent*, when erected, generally resembles the shanty-tent. It consists of a strip of canvas, having each end cut off to a point. The tent is pitched over three slanting poles, and the ends are brought down and securely pegged.

Another common tent may be described as the *simple*, or *tepee-tent*. It was much like the tepee of the Plains Indian, though usually much smaller and squatter. It usually consisted of four or five uprights lashed together at the top and covered with a wrapping of canvas or oiled cotton cloth.

Another simple shelter is the *lean-to tent*.

Should a storm arise all of a sudden—as so often happens in the mountains—a quick emergency shelter was often improvised by chopping a tree limb most of the way through, bending it to the ground, and hollowing out a refuge among the leaves.

CACHES

It often happened that trappers and traders were compelled, for want of transportation, to hide a portion of their pelts, stores, equipment, or other baggage. Such contingencies have given rise to a method of secreting articles called by the old French Canadian voyagers "*caching*."

Underground Caches

The proper place for citing an underground cache is in loose sandy soils, where the earth is dry and easily excavated. Near the bank of a river is the most convenient for this purpose, as the earth taken out can be thrown into the water, leaving no trace behind. When the spot has been chosen, the turf is carefully cut and laid aside, after which a hole is dug in the shape of an egg, big enough to contain the articles to be secreted. The earth, as it is taken out, is thrown upon a cloth or blanket, and carried to a stream or ravine, where it can be disposed of, being careful not to scatter any upon the ground near the cache. The hole is then lined with bushes or dry grass, the articles placed within, covered with grass, the hole filled up with earth, and the sods carefully placed back in their original position.

Another plan for making a cache is to dig the hole inside a tent and occupy the tent for some days after the goods are deposited. This effaces the marks of excavation. The mountain traders were formerly in the habit of building fires over their caches. Another method of caching is to place the articles in the top of an evergreen tree, such as the pine, hemlock, or spruce. The thick boughs are so arranged around the packages that they cannot be seen from beneath. Lash them to a limb and this will prevent them from being blown out by the wind. This will only work for articles that will not become injured by the weather.

Caves or holes in the rocks that are protected from the rains are also secure deposits for caching goods, but in every case care should be taken to obliterate all tracks or other indications of men having been near them. These caches will be more secure when made at some distance from roads or trail and in places where others would not be likely to pass.

To find a cache, a compass bearing and the distance from the center of it to some prominent object, such as a mound, rock, or tree, should be carefully determined and recorded, so that any one, on returning to the spot, will have no difficulty in ascertaining its position. If you have no compass, get a bearing by aligning two prominent objects.

SPLITTING LOGS

Logs are usually split by the use of wedges, but it is possible to split them by the use of two axes. To split a log with an axe, strike it smartly into the wood at the small end so as to start a crack, then sink the axe in the crack, A. Next take the second axe and strike it in line with the first one at B. If this is done properly, it should open the crack wide enough to release the first axe without trouble, which may then be struck in the log at C. In this manner it is possible to split a straight-grained piece of timber without the use of wedges. The first axe should be struck in at the smaller or top end of the log.

To split a log with wedges, take your axe in your left hand and a hammer or mallet in your right hand and, by hammering the head of your axe with the mallet, drive the blade into the small end of the log far enough to make a crack deep enough to hold the thin edge of your wedges. Make this crack all the way across the end of the log. Put two wedges into the log and drive them until the wood begins to split and crack along the sides of the log; then follow up this crack with other wedges, as shown at D and E, until the log is split in half.

BUILDING A TRAPPER'S LOG CABIN

It may be constructed of any size, but one of about twelve by ten feet (for an inside measurement) is large enough for most purposes.

Select straight logs, about a foot in diameter with the bark off. You will need about thirty-six to forty logs. Of these one-half should be fifteen feet in length and the other thirteen. These should be built up in a rectangular form, on a level piece of land. Look for ground that is slightly higher than the ground around it, as this will facilitate drainage.

If your house is not to be laid directly on the ground (called a *mudsill* construction), you may rest your bottom logs upon posts or stone piles; in either case, in the Northern States, these footings should extend three feet below the ground, so as to be below frost line and prevent the upheaval of the spring thaw from throwing the structure out of plumb.

Stake out the inside lines of the cabin.

Lay the ends of the logs over each other, and secure them
with notches at the corners. Cut each notch deeply enough to
allow the edges of the logs to meet. Lay the first tier of logs,
bracing them into position with stakes along the outside of the
proposed cabin.

If the cabin is to have a floor, cut three straight logs about
ten inches thick in their center and twelve feet long. Bed
these snuggly into the ground, one along each of the longer
walls and one in the center. They must be of an even height.
If one rests too high in spots, dress it with an axe or hatchet.
Planking the floor can be completed once the main structure is
accomplished.

Continue building the walls until all the logs are used, and
you will now have four sides, a little over six feet in height.

The place for the door should now be selected. The uppermost
log should form its upper outline and the two sides should
be cleanly and straightly cut with a crosscut saw. The window
openings, one or more, can next be cut, starting beneath
the second log from the top and taking in three beneath it.
Replace the logs above, and on the ends of those cut, in windows
and doors, proceed to spike a heavy plank, driving two nails into
each log, about five inches apart, one above the other. This will
hold them firmly in place and offer a close-fitting jam for the
door, as well as a neat receptacle for the window sashes.

The gable ends should next be built up on the smaller sides of the cabin. Start by laying a long log (notched as before) across the top of the structure at about two feet inside the edge. This should be done on both sides, after which they should be overlapped with logs at the corners.

Next lay two more long logs parallel with the first two and about a foot inside them, notching as before. The ends of these should be spanned with beams eight or so feet in length. Two more long logs are next in order—let them be one foot inside the last two. Overlap these with beams five and a half feet in length, and in the exact center of these last pieces chop notches for a heavy log for a ridgepole. The gable outline, direct from the ridgepole to the eaves, should now be cut off. This may be done either while the pieces are in position or the line may be marked, and the logs taken down in order to accomplish it.

The Cabin Roof

This may consist of either strips of bark or the rounded sides of logs split off and hollowed into troughs. The latter method is preferable, on account of its greater strength and durability, but the bark will answer the purpose very well and is much more easily obtained.

The first row is laid on with the hollow side up; securing them at top and bottom by nails driven through each into the ridge pole and eaves-log, care being taken that one of these pieces projects well over the gable, on both ends of the cabin. These pieces are now overlapped by the second row and with the addition of the large piece which covers them all at the ridge pole, the roof is complete and will stand a heavy rain with little or no leaking.

All crevices should now be stopped with moss, dried grass, or clay. When a bark roof is made, additional poles ought to be inserted beneath as props. They should be three or four inches in diameter and run parallel with the ridgepole at intervals on the slope, notched and nailed to secure them.

A chimney may be constructed if desired, but this necessity may be done away with by using a small camp stove and making a small opening in the gable end of the hut for the passage of the stovepipe. If a stove should not be at hand, you can build the fireplace and chimney as follows.

Log Rolling

In handling logs, lumbermen have tools made for that purpose: *cant-hooks, peevy irons, lannigans,* and numerous other implements with names as peculiar as their looks, but the old trappers and traders owned few tools but their tomahawks and axes, and the logs of most of their cabins were rolled in place by the men themselves pushing them up the skids laid against the cabin wall for that purpose. Two methods were used.

Pulling by Main Force

Take two ropes and fasten the ends securely inside the cabin.

Then pass the free ends of the ropes around the log, first under it and then over the top of it, then up to a team of men who, by pulling on the free ends, roll the log up to the top of the cabin.

Block and Tackle

Fasten a chain to each end of the log, and then fasten a pulley-block to the other side of the cabin. That is, the side opposite the skids and run the line through the pulley-block and back to a team of men, a horse or mule or a team of oxen. When the oxen were started, the log slid up the skids to the last completed log tier and muscled into place.

BUILDING A STONE CHIMNEY

Dig the foundation for your fireplace and chimney at least three feet deep; then fill the hole up with small, broken cobblestones until you have reached nearly the level of the ground. If you fail to dig this foundation the cold will work the ground under your chimney and the chimney will work with the ground, causing it to upset or to tilt to one side or the other.

In erecting the fireplace for your cabin, the stone-work should extend into the cabin itself, thus protecting the ends of the logs from the fire. It will be necessary to cut away an opening in the logs at the gable end, as was done for the door and windows. This should be about three feet square, and the fireplace should be built of stone and clay or mortar, to fill the opening and project inside the hut.

In gathering the stones for your chimney, remember that it makes no difference how rough and uneven it is on the outside. The more uneven the outside is the more picturesque it will appear, but the smoother and more even the inside is the less will it collect soot and the less will be the danger of chimney fires.

Nowadays we lay our chimney stones in cement, but in the era of the first mountain men, the mortar was most commonly a mixture of clay and fire ash.

See that each stone fits firmly in the bed and does not rock and that it breaks joints with the other stone below it. *Breaking joints* means that the crack between the two stones on the upper tier should fit over the middle of the stone on the lower tier; this, with the aid of the mortar, locks the stones and prevents any accidental cracks which may open from extending any further than the two stones between which it

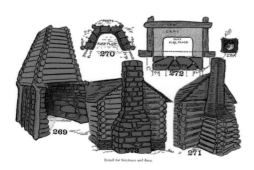

Detail for fireplaces and flues.

started. If, however, you do not break joints, a crack might run from the top to the bottom of the chimney causing it to fall apart. Above the fireplace make four walls to your chimney. Be certain the top of the chimney extends above the roof at least three feet; this will not only help the draught but it will also lessen the danger of fire.

Fill whatever gaps or spaces that may exist between the logs with a mixture of clay and moss.

Inside the cabin there will be plenty of room for the hanging of the skins and any number of cross-poles may be rested across the beams.

SOD HOUSE CONSTRUCTION

First erect two forked uprights and then steady them with two braces.

Next, lay four more logs or sticks for the side-plates with their butt ends on the ridge-pole and their small ends on the ground.

Support these logs by a number of small uprights—as many as may be necessary for the purpose. The uprights may have forks at the top or have the top ends cut wedge-shaped to fit in notches made for that purpose in the side-plates as shown by *A*.

The shortest uprights at the end of the roof should be forked so that the projecting fork will tend to keep the roof logs from sliding down. The roof is made by a number of straight rafters placed one with the butt in front, next with the butt in the rear alternately, so that they will fit snugly together until the whole roof is covered.

The sides are made by setting a number of sticks in a trench and slanting them against the roof; both sides, front and rear of the building, should project six inches above the roof in order to hold the sod and dirt and keep it from sliding off.

Up in the woods you must not expect to find green, closely cropped lawns or even green fields of wild sod in all places. Although in some parts the grass grows taller than a man's head, in other places the sod is only called so by courtesy; it normally consists of scraggy grass thinly distributed on gravel and sand, loose soil, and consequently the sod must be secured by having the walls project a little above the rafters all around the building.

During the summer this roof will leak, but then you can live in a tent; but when cold weather comes and the sod is frozen hard and banked up with snow, a sod house makes a good, warm dwelling.

KNOTS AND ROPE WORK

Before taking up the matter of knots in detail, it may be well to take a look at cordage in general. Cordage, in its broadest sense, includes all kinds of rope, string, twine, cable, etc., made of braided or twisted strands.

In making a rope or line (*A*) of hemp, jute, cotton, or other material the lines are loosely twisted together to form what is technically known as a "yarn" (*B*). When two or more yarns are twisted together they form a "strand" (*C*). Three or more strands form a rope (*D*), and three ropes form a cable (*E*).

To form a strand, the yarns are twisted together in the opposite direction from that in which the original fibers were twisted; to form a rope the strands are twisted in the opposite direction from the yarns of the strands, and to form a cable each rope is twisted opposite from the twist of the strands. In this way the natural tendency for each yarn, strand, or rope to untwist serves to bind or hold the whole firmly together.

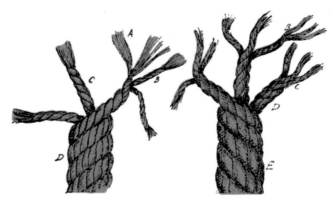

Rope is usually three-stranded and the strands turn from left to right or "with the sun," while cable is left-handed or twisted "against the sun" (*E*). Certain ropes, such as "bolt-rope" and most cables, are laid around a "core" (*F*) or central strand and in many cases are four-stranded

78

The strength of a rope depends largely upon the strength and length of the fibers from which it is made, but the amount each yarn and strand is twisted has much to do with the strength of the finished line.

Roughly, the strength of ropes may be calculated by multiplying the circumference of the rope in inches by itself and the fifth part of the product will be the number of tons the rope will sustain. For example, if the rope is 5 inches in circumference, 5 X 5 = 25, one-fifth of which is 5, the number of tons that can safely be carried on a 5-inch rope.

To ascertain the weight of ordinary right hand rope, multiply the circumference in inches by itself and multiply the result by the length of rope in fathoms (six feet) and divide the product by 3.75. For example, to find the weight of a 5-inch rope, 50 fathoms in length: 5 X 5 = 25; 25 x 50 = 1,250; 1,250 ÷ 3.75 = 333.33 lbs. These figures apply to Manila or hemp rope, which is the kind commonly used. Cotton rope is seldom employed except for small hand-lines, clothes-lines, twine, etc.

For ease in handling rope and learning the various knots, ties, and bends, we use the terms "standing part," "bight," and "end." The *Standing Part* is the longest part of the rope; the *Bight* is the part curved or bent while working or handling; while the *End* is that part used in forming the knot or hitch. Before starting work, the loose ends or strands of a rope should be whipped to prevent the rope from unraveling. It is a wise plan to whip the end of every rope, cable, or hawser to be handled.

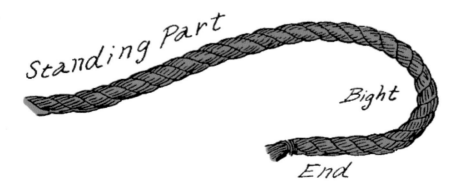

Standing Part

Bight

End

To whip a rope-end, take a piece of twine or string and lay it on the rope an inch or two from the end, pass the twine several times around the rope, keeping the ends of the twine under the first few turns to hold it in place, then make a large loop with the free end of twine, bring it back to the rope and continue winding for three or four turns around both rope and end of twine, and then finish by drawing the loop tight by pulling on the free end.

All knots are begun by loops or rings commonly known as necks.

These may be either overhand or underhand, and when a seizing or fastening of twine is placed around the two parts where they cross, a useful rope ring known as a *Clinch* is formed.

If the loose end of the rope is passed over the standing part and through the neck, you have made the simplest of all knots, known as the *Overhand Knot*.

The *Figure-Eight Knot* is almost as simple as the overhand.

Just a step beyond the figure-eight and the overhand knots are the *Square* and *Reefing knots*. The square knot is probably the most useful and widely used of any common knot and is the best all-around. It is very strong, never slips or becomes jammed, and is easily untied. To make a square knot, take the ends of the rope and pass the left end over and under the right end, then the right over and under the left.

Learn the simple formula of "left over right, and bring it under" then "right over left, and bring it under," and you will never make a mistake and form the despised *Granny*. The true *Reef Knot* is merely the square knot with the bight of the left or right end used instead of the end itself. This enables the knot to be "cast off" more readily than the regular square knot.

Neither square nor reef knots, however, are reliable when tying two ropes of unequal size together. For under such conditions they will frequently slip and sooner or later will pull apart. To prevent this, the ends may be tied or seized.

A better way to join two ropes of unequal diameter is to use the *Open-hand Knot*. This knot is quickly and easily made and never slips or gives, but it is rather large and clumsy.

The *Fisherman's Knot* is a good knot and is formed by two simple overhand knots slipped over each rope, and when drawn taut.

The *Ordinary Knot* is for fastening heavy ropes. It is made by forming a simple knot and then interlacing the other rope or "following around." This knot is very strong, will not slip, is easy to make, and does not strain the fibers of the rope. Moreover, ropes joined with this knot will pay out, or hang, in a straight line.

By whipping the ends to the standing parts it becomes a neat and handsome knot.

The *Weaver's Knot* is more useful in joining small lines, or twine, than for rope, and for thread it is without doubt the best knot known.

The ends are crossed, the end *A* is then looped back over the end *B*, and the end *B* is slipped through loop *C* and drawn tight.

This is a *Simple Hitch* within a loop, and is sometimes used in fastening two heavy ropes together. It has the advantage of being quick and easy.

When two heavy lines are to be fastened for any considerable time, a good method is to use the *Half-hitch and Seizing*. This is a secure and easy method of fastening ropes together and it allows the rope to be handled more easily and to pass around a winch or to be coiled much more readily than when other knots are used.

All the above knots are used mainly for fastening the two ends of a rope, or of two ropes, together. The knots used in making a rope fast to a stationary or solid object are known as "hitches" or "ties." One of the easiest to make and one which is very useful in fastening a boat or other object where it may be necessary to release quickly is the *Lark's Head*. To tie this, pass

a bight of your rope through the ring, or other object, to which you are making fast and then pass a marline-spike, a piece of wood, or any similar object through the sides of the bight and under or behind the standing part.

The end of the rope may then be laid over and under the standing part and back over itself. This knot may be instantly released by merely pulling out the toggle.

Almost as quickly made and unfastened is the *Slippery Hitch*.

To make this, run the end of the rope through the ring or eye to which it is being fastened, then back over the standing part and pull a loop, or bight, back through the *neck* thus formed. To untie, merely pull on the free end.

Two half-hitches—either around a post or timber or around the standing part of the rope—make an ideal and quickly tied fastening. To make these, pass the end around the post, ring, or other object, then over and around the standing part between the post and itself, then under and around the standing part and between its own loop and the first one formed. After a little practice you can tie this knot almost instantly and by merely throwing a couple of turns around a post, two half-hitches may be formed instantly. This knot will hold forever without loosening, and even on a smooth, round stick or spar it will stand an enormous strain without slipping.

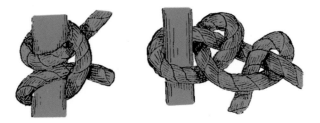

A more secure knot for this same purpose is the *Clove Hitch*. To make this, pass the end of rope around the spar or timber, then over itself, over and around the spar, and pass the end under itself and between rope and spar.

The *Tomfool Knot* can be used as handcuffs. If the hands or wrists are placed within these loops and the latter drawn taut, and the loose ends tied firmly around the central part, a pair of wonderfully secure handcuffs results.

Sheepshanks or *Dogshanks* are widely used for shortening rope, especially where both ends are fast, as they can be easily made in the center of a tied rope.

If a temporary halter is needed for a horse, this halter is made by putting the end of a long rope around the neck of the horse and then tying a common bow-line knot.

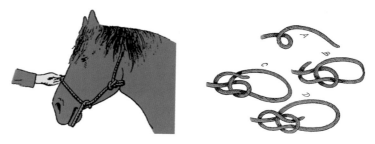

Next, pass the rope around the animal's head twice, then pass the second loop under the first.

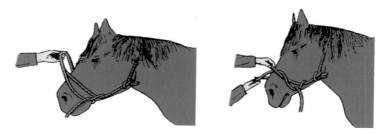

The rope should be sufficiently long enough to enable it to be passed over the ears of the animal.

It goes without saying that, you found yourself smack dab in the middle of the mountain wilderness, you'd have to learn to make do—and you can be very sure that the old-time trapper took his calories where he could get them—but given a supply of few staple items like salt, flour, sugar, cornmeal, coffee, tea and beans, the mountain man did very nicely when it came time to rustle up some grub. The wilderness was abounded with good things to eat, and game was plentiful. There was bear, buffalo, venison, moose, Rocky Mountain and big-horned goat, wild turkey, grouse, squirrel, rabbit, beaver, porcupine, and all manner of freshwater fish, turtles, and even frogs legs.

Regular cooking fire

—for making tea

for a bed of coals

FIRE BUILDING

There are nearly as many types or styles of campfire as there are fire builders—and most woodsmen have their own particular favorites—but a good rule of thumb is to design a fire that meets the exigencies of the situation in camp, keeping in mind the various imperatives of your planned cookery. For example: the ordinary method of fire building for heating an open-camp is to place it against a large green log or against a ledge of rock, a wall of stones built up artificially, or a pile of short green logs resting against two stakes that have been driven at a slight incline.

Fuel

A fire burns best when there are two short pieces of wood placed crosswise on the ground on which the fuel may rest and leave an opening for draft beneath. Green wood is best for holding fire, but it must be mixed with good dry wood or it will not burn well.

Standing dead trees are always drier than those that have fallen, unless the fallen trees are held up sufficiently above the ground to keep them well dried. Wood that is cut on low, damp ground is not as good as that found on higher places. These are the ones that usually pop and throw sparks into blankets, which can be quite the nuisance.

Almost all kinds of dry, hard wood burn readily and throw off plenty of heat. They also burn to embers and hard wood, and therefore should be selected when a bed of live coals is needed. Of the soft wood, dry pine and cedar burn freely but are consumed quickly, leaving no embers and making a lot of smoke. They are an excellent wood for kindling and for use in connection with green, hard wood. Green pine, cedar, fir, and tamarack burn slowly and require much dry wood to help keep them burning. White birch is excellent for camp-fires; dry or green and dry tamarack is one of the best of camp-fire woods.

There are various woods that answer well for kindling. Dry white pine, cedar shavings, and splints light readily, but dead "fat" pine is better. Pine knots that remain after the log has rotted away, when split, are heavy and yellow with dried pitch and if chopped into splinters, will burn like oil. An old pine log is often in the same condition, and if the camper can find any wood of this kind, he should take some to camp so that he will not need to hunt about for a suitable wood for starting a fire. The loose bark hanging to the white-birch tree trunks contains oil which causes it to take fire readily and burn with a bright flame.

While the woodsman invariably carries an axe with which to cut firewood, there may come a time when he has no axe and is obliged to camp out over night. Then getting together sufficient wood to keep fire over night is a real problem. Sometimes he can find a place where one tree has fallen across another, or if not, perhaps he can throw one over the other, and at the place where they cross he should build his fire. Then when the logs burn through he can move them and either keep shoving the ends into the fire as they burn away, or perhaps cross the pieces again and burn them into shorter and lighter pieces which can be handled readily.

Remember that flame naturally moves upward, so the wood should be lit from beneath. It is hard to get a fire started in any other way. Also remember that the wind drives the fire forward and you should light the wood under the windward side. The finest kindling should be placed first, then finely split dry wood on top, coarser wood on top of this, etc. The heavy wood should never rest too much on the kindling or the latter will be crushed into such a dense mass that it will not burn. Wood must never be placed so that the sticks fit closely together; a criss-cross or tepee style is much better.

Starting a Fire by the Bow Drill Method

To get wood into the proper condition for fire making by the friction method requires the selection of the proper kind of wood, and then a thorough drying indoors for weeks or even months. The wood must be as dry as wood can be, and such wood is never found in the forest. Only certain kinds of woods are really good for the purpose and among these kinds, cedar, balsam, and cottonwood seem to be the best. Spindle and block must be of the same kind of wood and equally dry.

The materials needed for making a fire are the bow, spindle, block, tinder, and a shell, a stone with a small cavity, or other similar object that can be used as a bearing or cap on top of the spindle. A mussel shell is the best natural object for the purpose, as it is light and has a hollow side that is smooth and makes an excellent bearing for the spindle end.

The bow, about two feet long, may be made of hickory or any springy wood, strung with stout, hard laid twine.

The spindle, made of any of the favorite woods, should be about sixteen inches long by three-fourths or one inch in thickness. The top should be rounded and the lower end shaped to a blunt, smooth point. It must be *very* dry.

The block should be an inch or a little more in thickness and of any width and length found convenient, but it should be large enough to be easily held down firmly with the knees when working the drill in the kneeling position. It really should be of the same kind of wood as the spindle.

The tinder may be any inflammable material—the mountain men called it *punk*—which can easily be fired from the burning dust, such as the shredded inner bark of a cedar tree, very dry and fine, mixed with shreds of white cotton cloth.

The operator cuts a V-shaped notch about three-quarters of an inch deep in the edge of the block. On the flat side of the block at the apex of the notch he then makes a small hole with the point of a knife as a starting place for the spindle.

Around this notch he places a small quantity of the tinder.

Then, giving the string of the bow a turn around the spindle, he kneels on the block, places the point of the spindle on the mark at the point of the notch, places the shell over the other end, and throwing his weight upon the spindle he works the bow back and forth quickly and steadily.

The spindle, revolving rapidly, bores its way down into the block, the dust that is worn from the block and spindle filtering down through the notch among the dry tinder. An increasing heat develops from the friction of the dry wood and soon an odor of scorching wood will be noticed; then a thin wisp of smoke arises from the dust in the notch and this grows stronger. After awhile the smoldering fire itself is visible in the dust which has accumulated in the notch and about the base of the spindle.

Here the operator stops the drill and blows the fire into flame. All that is necessary then is to place fine, dry twigs over the tinder and then coarser wood, and this wonderful feat of building a fire without matches is accomplished.

Flint and Steel as a Fire Starter

Matches are a comparatively recent invention. When this country was first settled, fires were generally made by means of flint and steel. By striking glancing blows with a steel object along the edge of a piece of flint, showers of sparks were thrown into a little pile of tinder to be blown into a flame by the fire-kindler. It is said that for an expert the trick was not at all difficult, and that fire could be produced very quickly; but it is obvious that very dry materials were necessary.

The Lens Method

But the easiest of all ways to make a fire without matches is by means of a magnifying glass or other lens. A reading glass, if the sun is bright enough, will produce a fire almost as quickly as it can be made with a match, providing, of course, that it is used the right way. In the absence of a reading glass, a watch or compass crystal, an eye glass, the lens from a field glass or camera, or even a clear glass bottle filled with a little water, may be used for concentrating the sun's rays onto a pile of tinder and thus producing a fire.

BRUNSWICK STEW

Take two large squirrels, one quart of tomatoes, peeled and sliced (if fresh), one pint of lima beans or butter beans, two teaspoonfuls of white sugar, one minced onion, six potatoes, six ears of corn scraped from the cob (or a can of sweet corn), half a pound of butter, half a pound of salt pork, one teaspoonful of salt, three level teaspoonfuls of pepper, and a gallon of water. Cut the squirrels up as a fricassee, add salt and water, and boil five minutes. Then put in the onion, beans, corn, pork, potatoes, and pepper, and when boiling again add the squirrel.

Cover closely and stew two hours, then add the tomato mixed with the sugar and stew an hour longer. Ten minutes before removing from the fire cut the butter into pieces the size of English walnuts, roll in flour, and add to the stew. Boil up again, adding more salt and pepper if required.

94

HOW TO MAKE THE BURGOO

Anything from an ordinary pail to one or many big caldrons, according to the number expected at the camp, will serve as vessels in which to serve the burgoo. The excellence of the burgoo depends more upon the manner of cooking and seasoning it than it does on the meat used in its composition.

If, for instance, we have a good string of grouse, we will take the legs and wings and necks for the burgoo and save the breasts for a broil, and if we have only a few grouse, we will put in a whole bird or two. We will treat the rabbits the same way, saving the body with the tenderloin for broiling. When cleaned and dressed, the meat of a turtle or two adds a delicious flavor to the burgoo; frog legs are also good with the other meat. Cut all the meat up into pieces that correspond, roughly speaking, to inch cubes; do not throw away the bones; put them in also. Even ill-smelling but palatable dried vegetables, will add immensely to the flavor of your burgoo. Put all the ingredients in the kettle, that is, unless you are using beans and potatoes as vegetables; if so, the meats had better be well cooked first, because the beans and potatoes have a tendency to go to the bottom, and by scorching spoil the broth.

Fill your kettle, caldron, or pot half full of water and hang it over the fire. While the water is getting ready to boil, get busy with your vegetables, preparing them for the stew. Peel the dry outer skin off your onions and halve them, or quarter them, according to their size; scrape your carrots and slice them into little disks, each about the size of a quarter, peel your potatoes and cut them up into pieces about the size of the meat, and when the caldron is boiling, dump in the vegetables. The vegetables will temporarily cool the water, which should not be allowed to again boil, but should be put over a slow fire where it will simmer. When the stew is almost done, add the salt and other seasonings. There should always be enough water to cover the vegetables. In a real burgoo we put no thickening like meal, rice, or other material of similar nature, because the broth is strained and served clear. Also no sweet vegetables like beets.

When the burgoo is done, dip it out and drink it from tin cups.

ROAST BEAVER TAIL

Roast beaver tail is considered a special delicacy. Many of the old wilderness men hang the flat trowel-like tails of the beaver for a day or two in the chimney of their shack to allow the oily matter to exude from it, and thus take away the otherwise strong taste; others parboil it as advocated for porcupine meat, after which the tail may be roasted or baked and the rough skin removed before eating.

BEAVER TAIL SOUP

Beaver tail soup is made by stewing the tails with what other ingredients one may have in camp; all such dishes should be allowed to simmer for a long while instead of boiling rapidly. As a man who was hunting in North Michigan once said:

> Although I am a Marylander, and an Eastern Shore one at that, and consequently know what good things to eat are, I want to tell you that I'll have to take off my hat to the lumber camp cook as the discoverer, fabricator and dispenser of a dish that knocks the Eastern Shore cuisine silly. And that dish is beaver-tail soup. When the beaver was brought into camp the camp cook went nearly wild, and so did the lumbermen when they heard the news, and all because they were pining for beaver-tail soup.

The cook took that broad appendage of the beaver, mailed like an armadillo, removed from it the underlying bone and meat, and from it made such a soup as never came from any other stock.

LUMBERMAN'S BAKED BEANS

Wash the beans first, then half fill a pail with them, put them over the fire, and parboil them until their skins are ready to come off—they are now ready for the pot. But before putting them in, peel an onion and slice it, placing the slices in the bottom of the bean pot. Now pour half of the beans over the onions and, on top of them, spread the slices of another onion. Take some salt pork and cut it into square pieces and place the hunks of pork over the onions, thus making a layer of onions and pork on top of the beans. Over this pour the remainder of the beans, cover the top of the beans with molasses. On the top of the molasses, put some more hunks of pork, add enough water to barely cover the beans. Over the top of all of this spread a piece of birch bark, then force the cover down good and tight.

Meanwhile a fire should have been built in the bean hole. When the fire has burnt to hot cinders, the cinders must be shoveled out and the bean pot put into the hole, after which pack the cinders around the bean pot and cover the whole thing with the dead ashes, or as the lumbermen call them, the black ashes.

If the beans are put into the bean hole late in the afternoon and allowed to remain there all night, they will be done in time for breakfast; the next morning they will be wholesome, juicy and sweet, browned on top and delicious.

A bean hole is not absolutely necessary for a small pot of beans. You can cook them in the wilderness by placing the pot on the ground in the middle of the place where the fire had been burning and then heaping the hot ashes and cinders over the bean pot until it makes a little hill, which you then cover with the black ashes and leave until morning.

HOW TO BARBECUE VENISON OR SHEEP

First dress the carcass and then stretch it on a framework of black birch sticks, for this sweet wood imparts no disagreeable odor or taste to the meat.

Next, build a big fire at each end of the pit, not right under the body of the animal, but so arranged that when the melted fat drops from the carcass it will not fall on the hot coals to blaze up and spoil your barbecue. Build big fires with plenty of small sticks so as to make strong red hot coals before you put the meat on to cook.

First bake the inside of the barbecued meat, then turn it over and bake the outside. To be well done, an animal the size of a sheep should be cooked at least seven or eight hours over an open fire. Baste the meat with melted bacon fat mixed with any sauce or sweet oil you may have or with nothing at all, for bacon fat itself is good enough for anyone. You might even use hot salt water.

HOW TO COOK VENISON

If you want to know how real wild meat tastes, drop a sleek buck with a shot just over the shoulder. Dress the deer and let it hang for several days; that is, if you wish the meat to be tender. Cut a steak two inches thick and fry some bacon, after which put the steak in the frying pan with the bacon on top of it and a cover on the frying pan. When one side is cooked, turn the meat over and again put the bacon on top, replace the cover and let that side cook. Serve on a hot plate and give thanks that you are in the open, have a good appetite, and that you are privileged to partake of a dish good enough for a king.

SOURDOUGH'S JOY

Slice bacon as thin as possible and place a layer over the bottom and around the sides of the Dutch oven like a pie-crust. Slice venison, moose meat or bear steak, or plain beef, medium thin and put in to the depth of 2½ inches, salting each layer. Chop a large onion and sprinkle it over the top, cover with another layer of bacon and one pint of water and place the lid on top. Fill the hole half full of hot embers, place the Dutch oven in the center, and fill the space surrounding the oven full of embers. Cover all with about 6 inches of dirt, then roll yourself up in your blanket and shut your eyes—your breakfast will cook while you sleep and be piping hot in the morning.

DOUGHGOD

First fry some bacon or boil it until it is nice and soft, then chop up the bacon into small pieces quite fine, similar to hash. Save the grease and set the bacon to one side; now take a pint of flour and half a teaspoon of salt, a spoonful of brown sugar and a heaping spoonful of baking powder, and mix them all while they are dry, after which stir in the water until it is in the form of batter; now add the chopped bacon and then mix rapidly with a spoon; pour it into a Dutch oven or a pan and bake; it should be done in thirty-five to forty minutes, according to the condition of the fire.

When your fire is built on a hearth made of stones, you might brush the ashes away from the hot stone and place your doughgod on it, cover it with a frying pan or some similar vessel, and put the hot cinders on top of the frying pan. You will find that it will bake very nicely and satisfactorily on the hearthstone.

In the old-fashioned open fire-places where our ancestors did their cooking, a Dutch oven was considered essential. The Dutch oven is still used, and is of practically the same form as that used by Abraham Lincoln's folks; it consists more or less of a shallow dish of metal, copper, brass, or iron, with four metal legs that may be set in hot cinders. Over that is a metal top which is made so as to cover the bottom dish, and the edges of the cover are turned up all around like a hat with its brim turned up. This is to hold the hot cinders which are dumped on top of it.

HOW TO DRY CORN

The pioneer farmers in America and many of their descendants up to the present time dry their Indian corn by the methods the early mountain men learned from the Indians. The corn drying season naturally begins with the harvesting of the corn, and it often continues until the first snow falls.

Selecting a number of ears of corn, the husks are pulled back exposing the grain, and then the husks of the several ears are braided together. These bunches of corn are hung over branches of trees or horizontal poles and left for the winds to dry.

Because of the danger from corn-eating birds and beasts, these drying poles are usually placed near the kitchen door of the cabin or sometimes in the attic.

SWEET CORN

There is a way to preserve corn which a few people still practice just as they learned from the Indians. First they dig long, shallow trenches in the ground, fill them with dried roots and small twigs, with which they make a hot fire and thus cover the bottom of the ditch with glowing embers. The outer husks of the fresh green corn are then removed and the corn is placed in rows side by side on the hot embers. As the husks become scorched the ears are turned over, and when browned on all sides they are deftly tossed out of the ditch by means of a wand or stick used for that purpose.

The burnt husks are now removed and the grains of corn are shelled from the cob with the help of a sharp-edged, fresh water clam shell.

The corn is then spread out on a cloth and allowed to dry in the sun. It is "mighty" good food, as any Southern born person will tell you. One can keep a supply of it all winter.

PARCHED FIELD CORN

Parch the field corn in a frying pan and then butter and salt it while it is still hot. You may parch field corn or sugar corn and crush or grind it after it has been parched. The knowledge of how to make the various kinds of corn bread and the use of corn generally from "roasting-ears" to corn puddings was learned from the American Indians.

ASH CAKES

Mix half a teaspoonful of salt with a cup of corn meal and add to it boiling hot water until the swollen meal may be worked by one's hand into a ball. Bury the ball in a nice bed of hot ashes (glowing embers) and leave it there to bake like a potato.

PONE

Pone is made by mixing the meal as described for the ashcake, but molding the mixture in the form of a cone and baking it in an oven.

PULLED FIREBREAD OR TWIST

The twist is made of dough and rolled between the palms of the hands until it becomes a long thick rope, then it is wrapped spirally around a dry stick or one with bark on it. The coils should be close together but without touching each other. The stick is now rested in the forks of two uprights, or on two stones in front of the roasting fire, or over the hot coals of a pit-fire. The long end of the stick on which the twist is coiled is used for a handle to turn the twist so that it may be nicely browned on all sides.

JOHNNY-CAKE

A Johnny-cake is mixed in the same way as the pone or ash cake, but it is not cooked the same, nor is it the same shape; it is more in the form of a very thick pancake. Pat the Johnny-cake into the form of a disc an inch thick and four inches in diameter. Have the frying pan plentifully supplied with hot grease and drop the Johnny-cake carefully into the sizzling grease. When the cake is well browned on one side, turn it and brown the other side. If cooked properly it should be a rich dark brown color and with a crisp crust. Before it is eaten it may be cut open and buttered like a biscuit, or eaten with maple syrup like a hot buckwheat cake.

FLAPJACKS

Put a large tin cupful of flour in a pan, add half a teaspoonful of salt, one heaping teaspoonful and one level teaspoonful of baking powder; mix the salt and baking powder well with the flour while it is dry. Then build your little mountain or volcano of flour with its miniature crater in the middle, into which pour water little by little; making the lava by mixing the dough as you go. Continue this process until all the flour is a fine batter; the batter should be thin enough to spread out rapidly into the form of a pancake when it is poured into the skillet or frying pan, but not watery.

Grease the frying pan with a greasy rag fastened to the end of a stick or with a piece of bacon rind. Remember that the frying pan only needs enough grease to prevent the cake from sticking to the pan; when one fries potatoes the pan should be plentifully supplied with very hot grease, but flapjacks are not potatoes and too much grease makes the cakes unfit to eat.

CAMP CORN BREAD AND CORN DODGERS

In the North they also call this camp corn bread "Johnny-cake," but whatever it is called, it is wholesome and nourishing. Take some corn meal and wheat flour and mix them fifty-fifty; add a teaspoon level full and a teaspoon heaping full of baking powder and about half a teaspoonful of salt; mix these all together, *while dry*, in your pan, then add water gradually. If you have any milk, go fifty-fifty with the water and milk, make the flour as thin as batter, pour it into a reflector pan or frying pan, prop it up in front of a quick fire; it will be heavy if allowed to cook slowly at the start, but after your cake has risen, you may take more time with the cooking. This is a fine corn bread to stick to the ribs. When made in form of biscuits, it is called "corn dodgers."

CAMP BISCUIT

Take two cups full of flour and one level teaspoonful and one heaping teaspoonful of baking powder and half a teaspoonful of salt and mix them together thoroughly while dry. To this you add milk and water—if you have no milk use straight water—mixing it as described for the flapjacks. Make the dough soft but stiff enough to mold with well floured hands, form it into biscuits about half an inch thick, put them into a greased pan, and bake them in any one of the ovens already described or by propping them up in front of the fire.

BOILED POTATOES

Almost anyone can cook potatoes, but few cook them well. Most people think the best way is to boil them in their jackets and to cook them perfectly in this manner is so simple and easy that the wonder is how anyone can fail. A kettle of screeching hot water with a small handful of salt in it, good potatoes of nearly equal size, washed clean and clipped at the ends, are requisites for this dish. Put the potatoes in the boiling water, cover tightly, and keep the water at high boiling pitch until you can thrust a sharp sliver through the largest potato. Then drain off the water and set the kettle in a hot place with the lid partly off. Take them out only as they are wanted—lukewarm potatoes are not good. They will be found about as good as potatoes can be, when cooked in their jackets. But there is a better way: select enough for a mess, of smooth, sound tubers; pare them carefully, taking off as little as possible, because the best of the potato lies nearest the skin, and cook as above. When done, pour the water off to the last drop; sprinkle a spoonful of salt and fine cracker crumbs over them; then shake, roll, and rattle them in the kettle until the outsides are white and floury. Keep them piping hot until wanted. This is the way to have perfectly boiled potatoes.

ROAST POTATOES

Many outdoor folk are fond of roast potatoes in camp; and they mostly spoil them in the roasting, although there is no better place than the campfire in which to do so. To cook them right, scoop out a basin-like depression in the fire, three or four inches deep, and large enough to hold the tubers when laid side by side; fill it with bright, hard-wood coals, and keep up a strong heat for half an hour or more. Next, clean out the hollow, place the potatoes in it, and cover them with hot sand or ashes, topped with a heap of glowing coals, and keep up all the heat you like. In about forty minutes, try them with a sharpened hardwood sliver; when this will pass through them they are done and should be raked out at once. Run the sliver through them from end to end to let the steam escape, and eat immediately, as a roast potato can quickly become soggy.

BEAN HOLE

The above illustration shows a half section of a bean hole lined with stones. The bean hole may, however, be lined with clay or simply the damp earth left in its natural state. In the bean hole the fire is built and burns until the sides are heated good and hot, then the fire is removed and the bean pot put in place, after which the whole thing is covered up with ashes and earth and allowed to cook at its leisure.

107

PORK AND BEANS

There is no article of food more easily carried, and none that contains more nourishment to the pound, than the bean. Limas are usually preferred, but the large white marrow is just as good. It will pay to select them carefully. Keep an eye on grocery stocks, and when you strike a lot of extra large, clean beans, buy twice as many as you need for camp use. Spread them on a table a quart at a time and separate the largest and best from the others. Fully one-half will go to the side of the largest and finest, and these may be put in a cloth bag and kept till wanted. Select the pork with equal care, buying nothing but thick, solid, "clear," with a pink tinge. Reject that which is white and lardy.

This is how to cook them: put a pound or more of clean pork in the kettle, with water enough to cover it. Let it boil slowly for a half an hour. In the meantime, wash and parboil one pint of beans. Drain the water from the pork and place the beans around it; add two quarts of water and hang the kettle where it will boil steadily—but not rapidly—for two hours. Pare neatly and thinly five or six medium sized potatoes and allow them from thirty to forty minutes (according to size and variety) in which to cook. They must be pressed down among the beans so as to be entirely covered. If the beans are fresh and fine, they will probably fall to pieces before time is up. This, if they are not allowed to scorch, makes them all the better. If a portion of pork be left over, it is excellent sliced very thin when cold, and eaten with bread. This makes a dinner for three or four hungry men.

BAKED BEANS

It is usually the case that some of the party will prefer baked beans. To have these in perfection, add one gill of raw beans and a piece of pork three inches square to the above proportions. Boil until the beans begin to crack open; then fork out the smaller piece of pork, place it in the center of your largest cooking tin, take beans enough from the kettle to nearly fill the tin, set it over a bright fire, invert the second sized tin for a cover, place live, hard-wood coals on top, and bake precisely as directed for bread. When the coals on top become dull and black, brush them off, raise the cover, and take a look. If the beans are getting too dry, add three or four spoonfuls of liquid from the kettle, replace cover and coals, and let them bake until they are of a rich light brown on top. Then serve.

BROWN BREAD

Brown bread and baked beans have a natural connection in the average American mind, and rightly so, as they supplement each other. But there is a better recipe for brown bread than is generally known—one that has captured the first prize at country fairs and won the approval of epicures across America. Here is the recipe; take it for what it is worth, but try it fairly before condemning it.

One quart of sweet milk, one quart of sour, two quarts of Indian meal and one quart of flour, and a cupful of dark, thin Porto Rico molasses. Use one teaspoonful of soda only. Knead thoroughly. Bake in a steady, moderate oven, for four hours.

CAMP SOUP

Soup is, or should be, a leading food element in every woodland camp. Soup requires time, and a solid basis of the right material. Venison is the basis, and the best material is the bloody part of the deer, where the bullet went through. We used to throw this away, but have learned better. Cut about four pounds of the bloody meat into convenient pieces and wipe them as clean as possible with leaves or a damp cloth, but don't wash them. Put the meat into a five-quart kettle nearly filled with water and raise it to a lively boiling pitch. Let it boil for two hours. Have ready a three-tined fork made from a branch of birch or beech, and with this test the meat from time to time; when it parts readily from the bones, slice in a large onion. Pare six large, smooth potatoes, cut five of them into quarters, and drop them into the kettle; scrape the sixth one into the soup for thickening. Season with salt and pepper to taste. When, by skirmishing with the wooden fork, you can fish up bones with no meat on them, the soup is cooked, and the kettle may be set aside to cool.

Squirrels—red, black, gray, or fox—make nearly as good a soup as venison, and better stews. Hares, rabbits, grouse, quail, or any of the smaller game birds may be used in making soup; but all small game is better in a stew.

MOUNTAIN MAN STEW

To make a stew, proceed for the first two hours precisely as directed for soup; then slice in a couple of good-sized onions and six medium potatoes. When the meat begins to fall from the bones, make a thickening by rubbing three tablespoonfuls of flour and two spoonfuls of melted butter together; thin to the consistency of cream with liquid from the kettle, and drip slowly into the stew, stirring briskly meanwhile. Allow all soups and stews to boil two hours before seasoning and use only the best table salt and white (or black) pepper. Season sparingly; it is easier to put salt in than to get it out. Cayenne pepper adds zest to a soup or stew, but, as some dislike it, let each man season his plate to his own palate.

FRIED SQUIRREL

Fried squirrels are excellent for a change, but are mostly spoiled by poor cooks who put tough old and tender young squirrels together, treating all alike. To dress and cook them properly, chop off the heads, tails, and feet with a hatchet; cut the skin on the back crosswise, and, inserting the two middle fingers, pull the skin off in two parts (head and tail). Clean and cut them in halves, leaving two ribs on the hindquarters. Put hind and fore quarters into the kettle, and parboil until tender. This will take about twenty minutes for young ones, and twice as long for the old.

When a sharpened sliver will pass easily through the flesh, take the hindquarters from the kettle, drain, and place them in the frying-pan with pork fat hissing hot. Fry to a light, rich brown. It is the only proper way to cook squirrel. The forequarters are to be left in the kettle for a stew.

VENISON STEAK

Venison steak should be pounded to tenderness, pressed, and worked into shape with a hunting-knife and broiled over a bed of clean hard-wood coals. A three-pronged birch fork makes the best broiler. For roast venison, the best portion is the forward part of the saddle. Trim off the flanky parts and ends of the ribs; split the backbone lengthwise, so that the inner surface may be well exposed; hang it by a strong cord or bark string in a powerful, even heat; lay thin strips of pork along the upper edge, and turn from time to time until done. It's better to be left a little rare than overdone. Next to the saddle for roasting comes the shoulder. Peel this smoothly from the side, using the hunting knife; trim neatly and cut off the leg at the knee; gash the thickest part of the flesh and press shreds of pork into the gashes with two or three thin slices skewered to the upper part. Treat it in the roasting as described above. It is not equal to the saddle when warm, but sliced and eaten cold, is quite as good.

JERKING MEAT

Fresh meat may be cured, or *jerked*, as it is termed in the language of the woodsman by cutting it into strips about an inch thick and hanging it in the sun, where in a few days it will dry so well that it may be packed in sacks and transported over long journeys without putrefying.

When there is not time to jerk the meat by this slow process, it may be done in a few hours by building an open frame-work of small sticks about two feet above the ground, placing the strips of meat upon the top of it, and keeping up a slow fire beneath, which dries the meat rapidly.

The jerking process may be done on the move without any loss of time by stretching lines from front to rear upon the outside of loaded wagons and suspending the meat upon them, where it is allowed to remain until sufficiently cured to be packed away. Salt is never used in this process and is not required, as the meat, if kept dry, rarely putrefies.

112

HOW TO DRESS SMALL ANIMALS

Dressing in this case really means undressing; taking their coats off and removing their insides. In order to prepare for broiling or baking any of the small fur-bearing animals, make yourself a skinning stick, using a forked branch; the forks being about an inch in diameter, make the length of the stick to suit your convenience—long enough to reach between the knees whether you are sitting on a log or squatting on the ground—sharpen the lower end of the stick and stick it into the ground, then take your coon, possum, squirrel, or muskrat, and punch the pointed ends of the forked stick through the thin place behind the heels of the small animal there sketched. Thus the hung animal may be dressed with comfort. If one is squatting, the nose of the animal should just clear the ground.

First take off the fur coat. To do this you split the skin with a sharp knife, beginning at the center of the throat and cut to the base of the tail, being careful not to cut deep enough to penetrate the inside skin or sack which contains the intestines; when the base of the tail is reached, use your fingers to roll back the skin. After the coat is removed and all the internal organs taken out, remove the scent glands from such animals as have them and make a cut in the forearms and the meaty parts of the thigh and cut out the little white things which look like nerves to be found there. This will prevent the flesh from having a strong or musky taste when it is cooked.

ROAST PORCUPINE

When a porcupine has been killed, it should be immediately thrown into the fire, there to remain until all the quills have been singed off of the aggressive hide, after which it may be skinned with no danger to the trapper from the wicked barbed quills.

After thoroughly singeing the porcupine, roll it in the grass to make certain that the burnt quills are rubbed off its skin, then with a sharp knife slit it up the middle of the belly from the tail to the throat, pull the skin carefully back, and peel it off. When you get to the feet, cut them off.

After it has been parboiled, suspend the porcupine by its forelegs in front of a good roasting fire, or over a bed of hot coals, and if well seasoned it will be as good a meat as can be found in the wilderness.

The tail particularly is very meaty and most savory; like beef tongue it is filled with fine bits of fat. Split the tail and take out the bone, then roast the meaty part.

Porcupine stuffed with onions and roasted on a spit before the fire is good, but to get the perfection of cooking it really should be cooked in a Dutch oven, a closed kettle, or an improvised airtight oven of some sort and baked in a bean hole or by being buried and baked deep under a heap of cinders and covered with ashes. Two iron pans that will fit together, that is, one that is a trifle larger than the other so that the smaller one may be pushed down into it to some extent, will answer all the purposes of the Dutch oven. Also two frying pans arranged in the same manner.

Always remember that after the porcupine is skinned, dressed, and cleaned, it should be *put in a pot and parboiled*, changing the water once or twice, after which it may be cooked in any way you like.

One method is to place it in the Dutch oven with a few hunks of fat pork; let the porcupine itself rest upon some hard-tack, hard biscuit or stale bread of any kind, which has been slightly softened with water.

On top of the porcupine lay a nice slice or two of fat pork and place another layer of soaked hard biscuit or hard-tack on the pork, put it in a Dutch oven and place the Dutch oven on the hot coals, put a cover on and heap the living coals over the top of it and the ashes atop that; let it bake slowly until the flesh parts from the bones. Thus cooked it will taste something like veal with a suggestion of sucking pig.

CAMP COFFEE AND TEA

For every cup of water allow one tablespoon of ground coffee, then add one for the pot. Use cold water and allow it to boil just once, and then remove from fire. Settle with ¼ cup of cold water. Serve hot.

Or bring water to a boil, and then add the ground coffee. Allow it to boil for five minutes, take it off the fire, let it settle and serve.

Tea

Allow one teaspoon of tea for every person, and one for the pot. Pour boiling water over the tea, set it aside in a warm place and allow it to steep for seven minutes. Never boil fresh tea but you may boil old tea leaves for three minutes and that will give you as good a brew as the first method.

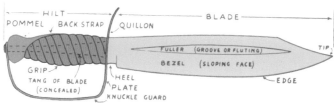

KNIVES

There's something almost mystical in the relationship between a man and his knife. Meriwether Lewis, upon realizing that he'd left his favorite dirk behind when he'd set out on his famous expedition, badgered President Jefferson to have it found and forwarded. President Jefferson, understanding this attachment between and man and his knife, took time to see that the dirk was sent along to the explorer.

A knife represents the simplest of all tools other than, perhaps, the base hammer. It comes in all sizes and shapes. It is a tool purpose-built to accomplish a particular task. It may be used to cut or slash or stab, pare, chop or skin, whittle or scalp. We think of a knife as *clever*, as it has so intimately to do with the work of our hands. Because of this, we also

117

understand it to be a reflection *on* and *of* its owner. You can tell a lot about a person by a quick look at his personal knife.

At the dawn of the golden age of the trapper, knives tended to be of a European pattern and manufacture.

The following are representations of several of the commonest types of knives used by the mountain men.

These are *killing* knives, intended for fighting and hunting.
Figure *a* is a war weapon and was nicknamed "Tecumseh's dagger."
Figure *b* is a British army dagger.
Figure *c* might be called an ordinary or common dagger.
Figure *d* is larger version of the common dagger.
Figure *e* is a "Hudson's Bay camp knife."
Figure *f* is an Indian dagger from Washington State.

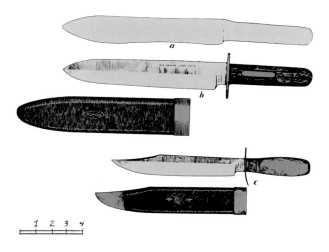

These are examples of standardized knives of the period.
Figure *a* is the rusted blade of a bowie knife.
Figure *b* is an intact rendering of the same knife.
Figure *c* is a smaller version of a bowie knife. This 8-inch
blade was frequently engraved and was much carried by city
dwelling easterners seeking a little of that mountain man mojo.

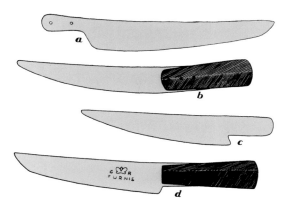

The above are representations of various trade knives of the
Northwest.
Figure *a* is a drawing of a handle-less, 11-inch butcher knife.
Figure *b* is another version of cheap butcher knife, a common
trade item.
Figure *c* represents a scalping knife blade.
Figure *d* is drawing of a British-made trade blade.

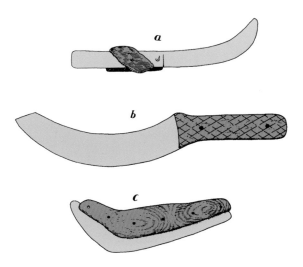

Figure *a* is an example of a tool made expressly for skinning.
Figure *b* appears to have been fashioned from the blade of a
circular saw.
Figure *c* represents the roughly shaped, dull-edged, iron
fleshing tool in common use among the trappers and traders of
the far west.

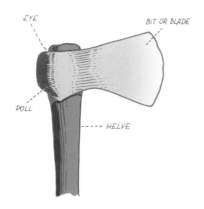

EYE

BIT OR BLADE

POLL

---- HELVE

A TRAPPER'S AXE

If any class of people need perfect tools, it is the class who must depend on them for their existence. The woodsman should have a perfect gun, perfect traps, perfect camp equipment, the best food he can buy, but above all he must possess a perfect axe.

It should be of the finest material and of the best temper, tough but not hard. When put to a great strain, steel will do one of two things: it will bend or it will break. If the axe-head is of good quality, with the proper proportion of carbon, it will stand an unusually severe test before it will do either. But when it does give, it should bend rather than break.

If the axe is tempered a little too hard, the edge will break when cutting into hard knots or frozen wood, and once the edge becomes dulled it is difficult to sharpen, for the trapper has no grindstone and must depend on file and whetstone to keep his cutting tools in condition. A hard axe cannot be filed.

The best axe heads are made of wrought iron, with welded steel bits. This gives maximum strength. The butt of the axe might also be of steel—and for the trapper—a claw for drawing trap staples. If the eye of the axe is not tempered, the entire head may be made of steel and will be almost, if not fully as strong.

The axe handle should be of sound, strong, straight-grained, springy wood; a broken axe handle can be as disastrous as a broken blade. The best wood for axe handles is good, second-growth hickory, but young white oak, the sapwood, is almost as good. Hard maple is also used extensively for axe handles, but it does not compare with hickory.

A proper trapper's axe should weigh only about two pounds—handle not included in the weight. This is heavy enough for practical purposes, while light to carry on the trail.

However, to make a light axe effective, it must have a long handle. The axe-handle should be from thirty to thirty-four

121

inches overall. With this tool you will be surprised to see what heavy work can be done.

One way to get a handle of the proper length is to remove the handle from a large axe and work it over into the proper shape and thickness.

Did you ever wonder why an axe handle is curved in an S shape?

The S shape of an axe-handle is made to fit the user's hands without strain on the arms or wrists. The curved shape permits a more solid hold when striking a blow than can be managed with a straight handle. The handle should be quite thick and "hand-fitting" near the end where it is grasped by the left hand (or right, according to whether the user is right or left handed), but the other part should be shaped so the hand can slide easily back and forth while chopping.

All this contributes to an efficient tool of light weight and of maximum chopping power; one that will sink easily into the tree, will burst the chip well, and will not bind in the wood.

THE WOODMAN'S PERFECT AX.

How to Fell a Tree with an Axe

There's considerable danger in the careless use of an axe.

In the woods it will really pay to be sure that there is not even the smallest twig in the way before you make a stroke with an axe. Trim all brush away from around a tree before you commence to cut it and follow the same precautions when you cut it into lengths or when lopping off the branches.

When cutting the fallen tree into lengths, the common and most convenient way is to stand on the log and chop it halfway through, between the feet, then turn it and cut the other side in the same way. Use double precaution when doing this. The smallest branch or sprout can turn the axe toward the foot of the chopper.

122

When chopping it down, the tree can nearly always be *thrown* in either of three ways—the way the tree inclines or to either side—but never in the opposite direction from its inclination.

Besides the inclination of the tree, the influence of the wind and the weight of the branches must also be considered. A good axe-man can throw the tree to any spot designated within the falling zone almost every time.

The wind is a great factor and must be considered, especially when it is strong or when the tree appears to stand perfectly straight. A tree on a slope that appears to be perpendicular will, in nearly every case, fall downhill if left free to fall, providing there is no contrary wind. If the tree really stands perfectly upright and there is no wind, it will usually fall toward the side that has the most branches—to the side having the greatest weight, if allowance be made for both wind and gravity. If he can estimate accurately the power of each of these forces, he can drop his tree exactly where he wants.

CUTTING THE FIRST NOTCH.

It's really very simple. In cutting a tree a first notch is cut on the side toward which the tree is to fall. Remember that this notch should be cut all the way into the center of the tree and, when finished, should be exactly at a right angle to the line on which the tree is to fall. A second notch is then cut on the opposite side, just a little higher on the tree, and when this notch is cut in almost to the center the tree will fall.

If the tree is notched to fall the way it inclines and there is nothing to prevent it going that way, the second notch should be cut exactly parallel to the first.

123

If the tree leans a little to one side—if there are more branches on that side or if the wind blows in that direction, the second cut should not be parallel with the first, but should be farther from it on the side from which the wind comes, so that there will be more wood to break on that side.

In no case should the notches entirely meet on the other side, because if they do—should the tree be cut entirely on one side—it will settle farther over to that side. Just how near you dare cut it off on the one side and how much you must hold on the opposite side can be learned only from experience.

There are other things that influence the *throw*. For instance, if there is nothing to interfere, the tree in falling will draw slightly toward the high side of the notch first cut. Also if the notch is not perfectly cut—if it is more acute on one side than on the other—as the tree falls, the top and bottom of the notch will meet on one side before they do on the other, and this is certain to swing the tree slightly toward the wide or obtuse side of the notch.

A heavy weight of branches, too, on one side may cause the tree to roll slightly in falling.

For safety, it is always best to get back some distance from the tree when it starts to fall, because if it falls over a rock, a log, or a little rise in the ground, the butt of the tree will kick and may take your head off.

If there are other trees in the way, look out for falling branches.

TOMAHAWKS AND HATCHETS

The following are examples of various types and styles of hatchets and tomahawks familiar to the trappers and traders of the beaver country.

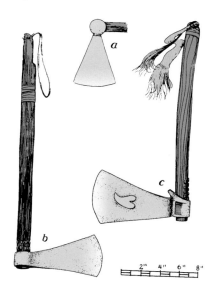

Figure *a* shows William Clark's drawing of the tomahawk design specified by the *Mandans*.

Figure *b* presents an *Osage* axe of an early—pre–Lewis and Clark—style.

Figure *c* is a copy of an *Ogallala* war hatchet.

Above are examples of three styles of spiked tomahawks. These types tended to be trade items but were also commonly used by the white trappers as well.

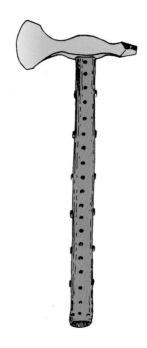

Above is a drawing of spiked tomahawk taken from the body of a *Sac* Indian. The haft is studded with brass tacks.

The hammer-hatchet was an ordinary trade item, used by every manner and class of mountain man.

BROADAX AND ADZ AND OTHER TOOLS

The broadax and the common adz have changed little over time and are still the best hand-tools for roughing out and shaping large pieces of wood, whether it be shaping a post, squaring a beam, or scooping out a dugout canoe.

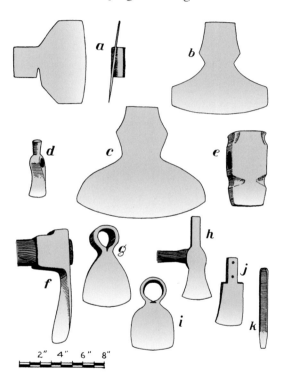

Figures *a, b, and c* are renderings of ordinary broadax blades of British make.

Figure *d* is shows a small hammer-hatchet head.

Figure *e* represents a heavy sledgehammer head.

Figure *f* is a rendering of a common carpenter's adz.

Figures *g* and *i* represent the heads of ordinary trade hoes.

Figures *h and J* are drawings of the heads of ice hatchets.

Figure *k* shows a common cold-chisel.

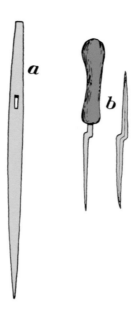

Though these iron tools were only inexpensive trade items, they were of real importance in the workaday life of the Native American. The trader made sure he was well supplied with these easily carried little tools and would often present them as little gifts.

SAWPITS AND TRESTLES

In an age before power tools, some version of the sawpit was an absolute necessity if you wanted to cut log into board. The idea was to maximize the cutting power of the two sawyers. In Europe and in the more or less crowded cities of eastern America, where the work was often done indoors and where space was at a premium, the tradition was to dig an actual pit in the floor of the shop. However, in rural America and out West, sawyers commonly worked from trestles. The problem was to get the logs up onto the trestle.

One answer to this was to build the trestle into a hillside, and then the logs could be rolled onto the frame.

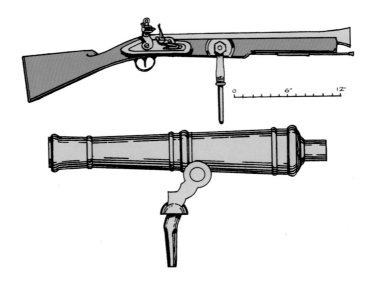

SWIVEL GUNS

In the Golden Age of the mountain man, swivel guns acted as the artillery of the trapper and trader. As they required a substantial and stable platform from which to operate, their uses tended to be defensive in nature. They were most often mounted on blockhouses or palisades, but were also frequently positioned in the larger of the watercraft, in keelboats, and pirogues.

The swivel-mounted blunderbuss above has a flared muzzle of about 2 inches in diameter and a barrel of 22 ½ inches in length. It fired ball, either as a single shot or as scattershot and buckshot.

The canon styled swivel gun, usually a one or two pounder, was 30 inches in length, with a bore of roughly 2 inches.

When loaded with powder only, it made an unholy boom when discharged and so proved useful in the firing of salutes, signals and farewells.

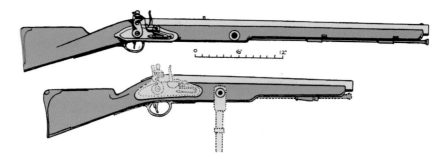

Another firearm of the period was the swivel-mounted musket, both long and short barreled. This 33-pound behemoth (top) was of English manufacture and was of a type commonly used by the Hudson's Bay Company.

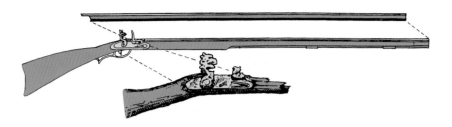

FLINTLOCK RIFLES OF THE MOUNTAIN MAN

The following are four examples of flintlock rifles most commonly employed by trappers and traders.

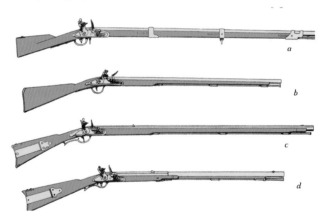

Figure *a* is an example of the *U. S. Musket*. Manufactured in 1795, it had a barrel 44 inches in length, threw a ball of just under one ounce, and was the standard firearm of the Lewis and Clark expedition.

Figure *b* represents a shortened version of the same essential firearm. Like the *U.S. Musket*, it fired either single ball or "fine shot," but was a lighter and—given its shorter length—more manageable weapon. Nicknamed the "fuzee," it was a favorite among the trappers, and often praised for its "elegance."

Figures *c* and *d* are examples of the *U. S. flintlock Kentucky rifle*. They featured barrels of 42 and 34 inches, respectively, and were greatly prized for their accuracy.

TRADE GUNS

The following illustrations represent firearms that were manufactured specifically for trade with the Native Americans. The comparatively low-priced musket of this class of firearm was apportioned much more widely than were the rifles of the period.

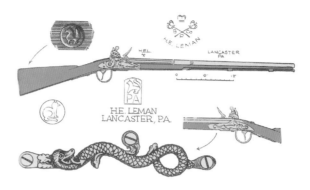

H. E. Leman of Pennsylvania was perhaps the best-known American manufacturer of guns for trade with the native peoples. His aim was to create an American gun that would rival the finest of British manufactured trade guns in both its quality as a weapon and in its decorative features.

Another standard trade gun was the *J. Henry*, both musket and rifle.

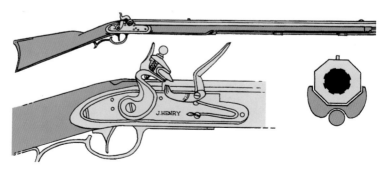

This gun featured a weighty 35-inch, eight-grooved, rifled barrel, and threw a .52 caliber ball. Though heavy and awkward to handle, the *J. Henry* was a popular trade item, due to its accuracy, and to the stopping power of its heavy shot.

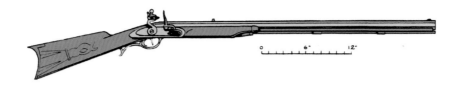

THE "PLAINS" RIFLE

The third decade of the nineteenth century saw the
introduction and the wide acceptance of a new class of rifle.
It went by a few different names; some people called it the
"plains rifle," others the "mountaineer's rifle," still others called
it simply the "short rifle." We know it today as the "Hawken,"
after the brothers Hawken—Jacob and Samuel, St. Louis
gunsmiths—who perfected it. The typical Hawken Plains rifle
had a heavy 34-inch octagonal barrel. It threw a .53 caliber
ball, was low sighted, with a second, or *set* trigger. Percussion
fired, it had an odd little steel basket (called a *snail*) that
enclosed the nipple, a half stock with a ramrod carried under
a metal rib. The butt stock was of a sturdy construction with a
crescent-shaped plate. Altogether it weighed in a 10 ½ pounds.
This proved to be the perfect gun for the mountain man, a
most dependable firearm, light enough and short enough to
be easily managed on horseback and throwing a ball-weight
sufficient to stop a buffalo or grizzly.

THE PISTOL

For reasons that must seem obvious, the pistol was a weapon much less commonly employed by the mountain man than was the musket or rifle. However there are numerous reports in journals describing its value as a weapon of "last resort."

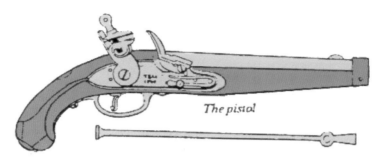

The pistol

BLACK POWDER

Gunpowder or *black powder*, as it was commonly known in the time of the mountain man, was a mixture of, roughly, 75 percent saltpeter (potassium nitrate), 15 percent charcoal, and 10 percent sulfur. Mixed and milled in the east, it was shipped west to the trading posts in lead boxes, which were then opened and the propellant apportioned into individual powder horns and flasks; the lead containers, in their turn, melted down for musket and rifle ball.

HOW TO MAKE A POWDER HORN

Powder horns were generally made from either cow or buffalo horn. The cow horn is a beige or cream color, the buffalo horn, a deep ebony color.

Begin by hack-sawing the base of the horn; removing the rough part of the horn where it had attached to the animal's head. Make the cut as near as possible to the perpendicular axis to the horn.

Next, rasp off the dry, scaly material that usually covers the lower or wider part of the horn. Finish this with a file and sandpaper, removing any rasp marks or gouges, working this until you have attained a uniform smoothness.

Turn now to drilling the spout hole. In order to prepare the end of the horn for drilling, cut off just enough of the tip so that there is sufficient thickness around the intended hole to seat the plug at the pouring end.

Drill the hole taking care not to drill through the side of the horn.

Fashion the spout plug so that it fits snuggly into the hole.

Return now to the completion of the butt plug. Cut a piece of board conforming to the inside measurements of the butt of the horn. Test it by tapping it into place. If the horn is irregular, heat the end of the horn by submerging it in boiling water and working it until you have the desired shape.

Once the horn has cooled, cut out its center and glue this inner plug into place. This hole will allow the horn to be charged with gunpowder.

For the outer portion of the butt plug, cut another piece of wood just slightly larger than the inner plug, so that it caps and extends just over the edges of the butt of the horn.

On the inside of this cap, glue a piece of wood conforming in size to the cut-out center of the inner plug and glue it into place. The goal is to set so that the plug may be removed to charge the horn, but when in place, it creates an air-tight seal.

Bevel or sand the outer edges of the butt plug to conform to your own individual esthetic.

Polish and decorate the powder horn as you will.

THE BISON OR *AMERICAN BUFFALO* BY MAYNE REID

The bison—universally though wrongly called *buffalo*—is the largest ruminant indigenous to the Americas, and perhaps the most interesting animal in America. Its great size and strength—the prodigious numbers in which it was found; its peculiar *habitat*; the value of its flesh and hide to the hunter; the mode of its chase and capture; all these circumstances render the buffalo an interesting and highly-prized animal.

The appearance of the animal is well-known—the enormous head, with its broad triangular front, the conical hump on the shoulders, the small but brilliantly piercing eyes, the short black horns of crescent shape, the profusion of shaggy hair about the neck and foreparts of the body, the disproportioned bulk of the smaller hind-quarters, the short tail, with its tufted extremity. The hind-quarters are covered with a much shorter and smoother coat of hair, which adds to their apparent disproportion, and this, with the long hirsute covering of the breast, neck, hump, and shoulders, gives to the buffalo—especially when seen in a picture—a somewhat lion-like figure. The naked tail, with its tuft at the end, strengthens this similarity.

Some of these characteristics belong only to the bull. The cow is less shaggy in front, has a smaller head, a less fierce appearance, and is altogether more like the common black cattle.

The buffalo is of a dark brown color—sometimes nearly black—and sometimes of a burnt or liver hue; but this change depends on the season. The young coat of hair is darker, but changes as the season advances. In autumn it is nearly black, and then the coat of the animal has a shiny appearance; but as winter comes on and the hair lengthens, it becomes lighter and more bleached-like. In the early part of summer it has a yellowish brown hue and, at this time, with rubbing and wallowing, part of it has already come off, while large flakes hang ragged and loose from the flanks, ready at any moment to drop off.

In size, the American buffalo competes with the European species (*Bos aurochs*), now nearly extinct. These animals differ in shape considerably, but the largest individuals of each species would very nearly balance one another in weight. Either of them is equal in size and weight to the largest specimens of the common ox.

A full-grown buffalo-bull is six feet high at the shoulders, eight feet from the snout to the base of the tail, and will weigh about 1,500 pounds. The flesh of the buffalo is juicy and delicious, equal, indeed superior, to well-fed beef. It may be regarded as beef with a *game flavor*. Many people—trappers and hunters—prefer it to any other species of meat.

The flesh of the cow is more tender and savory than that of the bull; and in a hunt when "meat" is the object, the cow is selected as a mark for the arrow or bullet. The parts most esteemed are the tongue, the "hump-ribs" (the long spinous process of the first dorsal vertebra), and the marrow of the shank bones. "Boudins" (part of the intestines) are also favorite "tit-bits" among Indians and trappers.

The tongue, when dried, is superior to those of common beeves, and, indeed, the same may be said of the other parts, but there is a better and worse in buffalo-beef, according to the age and sex of the animal. "Fat cow" is a term for the super-excellent, and by "poor bull," or "old bull," is meant a very unpalatable article, only to be eaten by the hunter in times of necessity.

One of the most singular facts in relation to the buffalo is their enormous numbers. Nothing but the vast extent of their pasturage could have sustained such droves as have from time to time been seen. Thousands frequently feed together, and the plain for miles is often covered with a continuous drove. Sometimes they are seen strung out into a long column, passing from place to place, and roads exist made by them that resemble great highways. Sometimes these roads, worn by the rains, form great hollows that traverse the level plain, and they often guide the thirsty hunter in the direction of water.

Another curious fact about the buffalo is their habit of wallowing. The cause of this is unclear. It may be that they are prompted to it, as swine are, partly to cool their blood by bringing their bodies in contact with the colder earth, and partly to scratch themselves as other cattle do, and free their skins from the annoying insects and parasites that prey upon them. It must be remembered that in their pasturage no trees or "rubbing posts" are to be found, and in the absence of these they are compelled to resort to wallowing. They fling themselves upon their sides and, using their hunch and shoulder as a pivot, spin round and round for hours at a time. In this rotatory motion they aid themselves by using their legs freely. The earth becomes hollowed out and worn into a circular basin, often of considerable depth, and this is known as a "buffalo wallow." Such curious circular concavities are seen wherever these animals range, sometimes grown over with grass, sometimes freshly hollowed out, and not infrequently containing water, with which the hunter assuages his thirst, and so, too, the buffalo themselves. This has led to the fanciful idea of the early explorers that there existed on the American Continent an animal that *dug its own wells!*

Buffalo hunting is not without peril. The hunter frequently risks his life; and numerous have been the fatal results of encounters with these animals. The bulls, when wounded, cannot be approached, even on horseback, without considerable risk. The buffalo runs with a gait apparently heavy and lumbering—first heaving to one side, then to the other, like a ship at sea; but this gait, although not equal in speed to that of a horse, is far too fast for a man on foot, and the swiftest runner, unless favored by a tree or some other object, will be surely overtaken, and either gored to death by the animal's horns, or pounded to a jelly under its heavy hoofs.

MULE DEER HUNTING

The mountain man most often hunted the mule deer, which is the subspecies most prevalent in the western mountains of America, and is distinguished by its mule-like ears.

Deer Hunting Tips

One of the great tricks of deer hunting is knowing how to approach the game without being spotted. This is not easily managed unless the hunter sees the deer before he is himself discovered. There are many things in the woods that so resemble the deer in color that none but a practiced eye can often detect the difference.

When the deer is at rest, it generally turns its head from the wind, from which position it can see any predator approaching from that direction. It counts on its nose to inform it of the presence of danger from the opposite side. Therefore, the best method of hunting deer is *across the wind*.

The best time to stalk deer is when they are feeding, either early in the morning or just before dark.

Advance cautiously, keeping your eyes on the deer, and if possible screening yourself behind intervening rocks, trees, or other features of the landscape. In the absence of this cover, crawl along on your hands and knees in the grass. If the deer hears you, stay motionless and absolutely still. Its vision is its keenest sense, but if the hunter does not move, the deer will, after a short time, recover from its alarm and resume grazing, when it may be approached again. The deer always exhibits alarm by a sudden jerking of the tail just before it raises its head.

Many men, upon suddenly encountering a deer are seized with a nervous excitement commonly called "*buck fever*," which causes them to fire off a shot quickly. Most often this results in a miss, a shot too high. Force yourself to take your shot deliberately, sighting your rifle low, or don't take the shot at all.

BIG HORN SHEEP

The big-horn or mountain sheep has a body like the deer, with the head of a sheep, surmounted by an enormous pair of short, heavy horns. It is found throughout the Rocky Mountains, and hides out on the most inaccessible peaks and in the wildest and least-frequented glens. It clambers over almost perpendicular cliffs with the greatest of ease and celerity, skipping from rock to rock, and cropping the tender herbage that grows on them.

Folks used to explain that this animal leaped from crag to crag, landing on his horns—and that this is why the front of the horns are much battered. But it is very common to see horns that have no bruises on them, and old mountaineers tell of seeing the bucks engaged in desperate encounters with their huge horns, which, in striking together, made loud reports. This no doubt accounts for the marks sometimes seen on them.

The animal is gregarious, but it's rare that more than eight or ten are found in a flock. When not grazing they seek the sheltered sides of the mountains and rest among the rocks.

The flesh of the big-horn, when fat, is said to be more tender, juicy, and delicious than that of any other game animal—darn good eating!

HUNTING THE BIG-HORN.

144

HUNTING THE BIG HORN

In its habits the big horned mountain sheep very much resembles the chamois of the Swiss Alps, and is hunted in much the same manner.

The hunter must maneuver across the most inaccessible and broken ground and approach with great caution, because the big horn tends to be uncommonly skittish. The least unusual noise causes it to flit away like a phantom and, once spooked, it will be seen no more. When you can manage it, always approach from above. The big horn's ability to get itself to the highest ground is its chief defense, and so it is less wary of danger from above. As usual, watch your wind and in taking your shot, aim low.

GRIZZLY BEAR

It is one thing to do the deed, to hunt and get your bear. It is quite another thing to tell everybody all about it round the campfire at the rendezvous.

Old Pinto by Allan Kelly

This is an incredible bear story, but it is true. George Gleason told it to a man who knew the bear so well that he thought the old Pinto Grizzly belonged to him and wore his brand, and as George is no bear hunter himself, but is a plain, ordinary, truthful person, there is not the slightest doubt that he related only the facts. George said some of the facts were incredible before he started in. He had never heard or read of such tenacity of life in any animal. But there are precedents, even if George never heard of them.

The vitality of the California Grizzly is astonishing, as many a man has sorrowful reason to know, and the tenacity of the Old Pinto's hold on life was remarkable, even among Grizzlies. This Pinto was a famous bear. His home was among the rocks and manzanita thickets of La Liebra Mountain, a limestone ridge southwest of Tehachepi that divides Gen. Beale's two ranches, Los Alamos y Agua Caliente and La Liebra, and his range was from Tejon Pass to San Emigdio. His regular occupation was killing Gen. Beale's cattle, and the slopes of the hills and the *cienegas* around Castac Lake were strewn with the bleached bones of his prey. For twenty years that solitary old bear had been monarch of all that Gen. Beale surveyed—to paraphrase President Lincoln's remark to Surveyor-General Beale himself—and wrought such devastation on the ranch that for years there had been a standing reward for his hide.

Men who had lived in the mountains and knew the old Pinto's infirmity of temper were wary about invading his domains, and not a vaquero could be induced to go afoot among the manzanita thickets of the limestone ridge. The man who thought he owned the Pinto followed his trail for two months many years ago and learned many things about him; among others that the track of his hind foot measured fourteen inches in length and nine inches in width; that the hair on his head and shoulders was nearly white; that he could break a steer's neck with a blow of his paw; that he feared neither man nor his works; that while he would invade a camp with leisurely indifference, he would not enter the stout oak-log traps constructed for his capture; and finally, that it would be suicide to meet him on the trail with anything less efficient than a Gatling gun.

Old Juan, the vaquero, who lived in a cabin on the flat below the alkaline pool called Castac Lake, was filled with a fear of Pinto that was akin to superstition. He told how the bear had followed him home and besieged him all night in the cabin, and he would walk five miles to catch a horse to ride two miles in the hills. To him old Pinto was "mucho diablo," and a shivering terror made his eyes roll and his voice break in trembling whispers when he talked of the bear while riding along the cattle trails. Once upon a time an ambitious sportsman of San Francisco, who wanted to kill something bigger than a duck and more ferocious than a jackrabbit, read about Pinto and persuaded himself that he was bear-hunter enough to tackle the old fellow. He went to Fort Tejon, hired a guide and made an expedition to the Castac. The guide took the hunter to Spike-buck Spring, which is at the head of a ravine under the limestone ridge, and showed to him the footprints of a big bear in the mud and along the bear trail that crosses the spring. One glance at the track of Pinto's foot was sufficient to dispel all the dime-novel day dreams of the sportsman and start a readjustment of his plan of campaign. After gazing at that foot-print, the slaying of a Grizzly by "one well-directed shot" from the "unerring rifle" was a feat that lost its beautiful simplicity and assumed heroic proportions. The man from San Francisco had intended to find the bear's trail, follow it on foot, overtake or meet the Grizzly and kill him in his tracks, after the manner of the intrepid hunters that he had read about, but he sat down on a log and debated the matter with the guide. That old-timer would not volunteer advice, but when it was asked he gave it, and he told the man from San Francisco that if he wanted to tackle a Grizzly all by his lonely self, his best plan would be to stake out a calf, climb a tree and wait for the bear to come along in the night.

So the man built a platform in the tree, about ten feet from the ground, staked out a calf, climbed up to the platform and waited. The bear came along and killed the calf, and the man in the tree saw the lethal blow, heard the bones crack and changed his plan again. He laid himself prone upon the platform, held his breath and hoped fervently that his heart would not thump loudly enough to attract the bear's intention. The bear ate his fill of the quivering veal, and then reared on his haunches to survey the surroundings. The man from San Francisco solemnly assured the guide in the morning, when he got back to camp, that when Pinto sat up he actually looked down on that platform and could have walked over to the tree and picked him off like a ripe persimmon, and he thanked heaven devoutly that it did not come into Pinto's head that that would be a good thing to do. So the man from San Francisco broke camp and went home with some new and valuable ideas about hunting Grizzlies, chief of which was the very clear idea that he did not care for the sport.

This is the sort of bear Old Pinto was, eminently entitled to the name that Lewis and dark applied to his tribe—Ursus Ferox. Of course he was called "Old Clubfoot" and "Reelfoot" by people who did not know him, just as every big Grizzly has been called in California since the clubfooted-bear myth became part of the folk lore of the Golden State, but his feet were all sound and whole. The Clubfoot legend is another story and has nothing to do with the big bear of the Castac.

Pinto was a "bravo" and a killer, a solitary, cross-grained, crusty-tempered old outlaw of the range. What he would or might do under any circumstances could not be predicated upon the basis of what another one of his species had done under similar circumstances. The man who generalizes the conduct of the Grizzly is liable to serious error, for the Grizzly's individuality is strong and his disposition various. Because one Grizzly scuttled into the brush at the sight of a man, it does not follow that another Grizzly will behave similarly. The other Grizzly's education may have been different. One bear lives in a region infested only by small game, such as rabbits, wood-mice, ants and grubs, and when he cannot get a meal by turning over flat rocks or stripping the bark from a decaying tree, he digs roots for a living. He is not accustomed to battle and he is not a killer, and he may be timorous in the presence of man. Another Grizzly haunts the cattle or sheep ranges and is accustomed to seeing men and beasts flee before him for their lives. He lives by the strong arm, takes what he wants like a robber baron, and has sublime confidence in his own strength, courage and agility. He has killed bulls in single combat, evaded the charge of the cow whose calf he has caught, stampeded sheep and their herders. He is almost exclusively carnivorous and consequently fierce. Such a bear yields the trail to nothing that lives. That is why Old Pinto was a bad bear.

So long as Pinto remained in his dominions and confined his maraudings to the cattle ranges, he was reasonably safe from the hunters and perfectly safe from the settler and his strychnine bottle, but for some reasons of his own he changed his habits and his diet and strayed over to San Emigdio for mutton. Perhaps, as he advanced in years, the bear found it more difficult to catch cattle, and having discovered a band of sheep and found it not only easy to kill what he needed, but great fun to charge about in the band and slay right and left in pure wanton ferocity, he took up the trade of sheep butcher. For two or three years he followed the flocks in their summer grazing over the vast, spraddling mesas of Pine Mountain, and made a general nuisance of himself in the camps. There have been other bears on Pine Mountain, and the San Emigdio flocks have been harassed there regularly, but no such bold marauder as Old Pinto ever struck the range. Other bears made their forays in the night and hid in the ravines during the day, but Pinto strolled into the camps at all hours, charged the flocks when they were grazing and stampeded Haggin and Carr's merinos all over the mountains.

The herders, mostly Mexicans, Basques and Portuguese, found it heart-breaking to gather the sheep after Pinto had scattered them, and moreover they were mortally afraid of the big Grizzly and took to roosting on platforms in the trees instead of sleeping in their tents at night. Worse than all else, the bear killed their dogs. The men were instructed by the boss of the camp to let the bear alone and keep out of his way, as they were hired to herd sheep and not to fight bears, but the dogs could not be made to understand such instructions and persisted in trying to protect their woolly wards.

The owners were accustomed to losing a few hundred sheep on Pine Mountain every summer, and figured the loss in the fixed charges, but when Pinto joined the ursine band that followed the flocks for a living, the loss became serious and worried the majordomo at the home camp. So another reward was offered for the Grizzly's scalp and the herders were instructed to notify the Harris boys at San Emigdio whenever the bear raided their flocks.

Here is where Gleason's part of the story begins. The bear attacked a band of sheep one afternoon, killed four and stampeded the Mexican herder, who ran down the mountain to the camp of the Harris boys, good hunters who had been engaged by the majordomo to do up Old Pinto. Two of the Harris boys and another man went up to the scene of the raid, carrying their rifles, blankets and some boards with which to construct a platform. They selected a pine tree and built a platform across the lower limbs about twenty feet from the ground. When the platform was nearly completed, two of the men left the tree and went to where they had dropped their blankets and guns, about a hundred yards away. One picked up the blankets and the other took the three rifles and started back toward the tree, where the third man was still tinkering the platform. The sun had set, but it was still twilight, and none of the party dreamed of seeing the bear at that time, but within forty yards of the tree sat Old Pinto, his head cocked to one side, watching the man in the tree with much evident interest. Pinto had returned to his muttons, but found the proceedings of the man up the tree so interesting that he was letting his supper wait.

The man carrying the blankets dropped them and seized a heavy express rifle that some Englishman had left in the country. The other man dropped the extra gun and swung a Winchester 45-70 to his shoulder. The express cracked first, and the hollow-pointed ball struck Pinto under the shoulder. The 45-70 bullet struck a little lower and made havoc of the bear's liver. The shock knocked the bear off his pins, but he recovered and ran into a thicket of scrub oak. The thicket was impenetrable to a man, and there was no man present who wanted to penetrate it in the wake of a wounded Grizzly.

The hunters returned to their camp, and early next morning they came back up the mountain with three experienced and judicious dogs. They had hunted bears enough to know that Pinto would be very sore and ill-tempered by that time, and being men of discretion as well as valor, they had no notion of trying to follow the dogs through the scrub oak brush. Amateur hunters might have sent the dogs into the brush and remained on the edge of the thicket to await developments, thereby involving themselves in difficulties, but these old professionals promptly shinned up tall trees when the dogs struck the trail. The dogs roused the bear in less than two minutes, and there was tumult in the scrub oak. Whenever the men in the trees caught a glimpse of the Grizzly they fired at him, and the thud of a bullet usually was followed by yells and fierce growlings, for the bear is a natural sort of a beast and always bawls when he is hurt very badly. There is no affectation about a Grizzly, and he never represses the instinctive expression of his feelings. Probably that is why Bret Harte calls him "coward of heroic size," but Bret never was very intimately acquainted with a marauding old ruffian of the range.

The hunters in the trees made body shots mostly. Twice during the imbroglio in the brush the bear sat up and exposed his head and the men fired at it, but as he kept wrangling with the dogs, they thought they missed. This is the strange part of the story, for some of the bullets passed through the bear's head and did not knock him out. One Winchester bullet entered an eye-socket and traversed the skull diagonally, passing through the forward part of the brain. A Grizzly's brain-pan is long and narrow, and a bullet entering the eye from directly in front will not touch it. Wherefore it is not good policy to shoot at the eye of a charging Grizzly. Usually it is equally futile to attempt to reach his brain with a shot between the eyes, unless the head be in such a position that the bullet will strike the skull at a right angle, for the bone protecting the brain in front is from two and a half to three inches thick, and will turn the ordinary soft bullet. One of the men did get a square shot from his perch at Pinto's forehead, and the 45-70-450 bullet smashed his skull.

The shot that ended the row struck at the "butt" of the Grizzly's ear and passed through the base of the brain, snuffing out the light of his marvelous vitality like a candle. Then the hunters came down from their roosts, cut their way into the thicket and examined the dead giant. Counting the two shots fired the night before, one of which had nearly destroyed a lung, there were eleven bullet holes in the bear, and his skull was so shattered that the head could not be saved for mounting. Only two or three bullets bad lodged in the body, the others having passed through, making large, ragged wounds and tearing the internal organs all to pieces.

The skin, which weighed over one hundred pounds, was taken to Bakersfield, and the meat that had not been spoiled by bullets was cut up and sold to butchers and others. Estimating the total weight from the portions that were actually tested on the scales, the butchers figured that Pinto weighed 1100 pounds. The 1800- and 2000-pound bears have all been weighed by the fancy of the men who killed them, and the farther away they have been from the scales the more they have weighed.

All furs are best in winter, but trapping can be carried on for at least six months of the year—really any time between the first of October and the middle of April. From the first of May until the middle of September, trapping is not pursued as the furs are worth little because the animals have, on the whole, shed their coats. As autumn approaches the new growth appears, and the fur becomes thick and glossy. By the middle of October most furs are in their prime, but the heart of winter is the best time for general trapping. The furs of the mink, muskrat, fisher, marten, and beaver are not in their perfect prime until this season. And all other furs are sure to be in good condition at this time as well.

SNARES

In the early days before the steel trap came into general use, the snare was used almost exclusively for the capture of the fur-bearers. However, deadfalls and snares are good traps for

155

certain animals and it is well to know how to make and use them for one may sometimes see a good place in which to place a trap but may not have a steel trap along. In such cases the knowledge of how to construct a practical deadfall may be of value. It is true that many of the fur-bearing animals are too cunning to be captured by such a contrivance, but some of the most wary fall easy victims to the snare. Some of the most expert fox trappers use the snare in preference to the steel trap, but this number is comparatively small.

The Common Snare

The common snare is composed of three pieces, all to be cut from a shingle or thin board. The first should be about eight inches long and three-quarters of an inch in width. This is for the upright. An oblong mortise should be cut through this piece, one inch in length, and beginning at about an inch from the end of the stick. Three inches from the other end, and on one of the broad sides of the stick, a notch should be made.

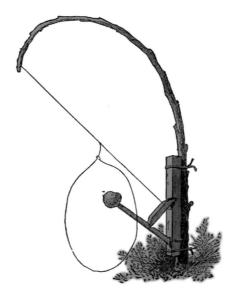

The bait stick should be four or five inches long, one end fitting easily into the mortise, where it should be secured by a line, or smooth nail driven through so as to form a hinge on which it will work easily. On the upper side of this stick and two inches from the pivot, a notch should be cut, similar to that in the upright. The catch piece should be about two inches in length and beveled off to a flat edge at each end.

To set the snare, it is only necessary to find some stout sapling, upon which the upright stick may be attached to it close to the ground, lashed firmly around both. It is a good idea to cut slight grooves at each end of the upright for the reception of the lashings, in order to prevent slipping. Tie a strong piece of line around one end of the catch piece, knotting it on the beveled side. Cut the line about two feet in length and attach the other end to the tip of the sapling. Adjust the bait stick on its pivot. Now lower the catch piece and lodge the knotted end beneath the notch in the upright and the other end in the notch on the bait stick. Take care to set the catch pieces deftly in the notches, in order to insure sensitiveness. At about four inches from the catch piece, the wire noose should be attached and arranged in a circle directly around the bait. Back up the trap with a few sticks to prevent the bait from being approached from behind, and the thing is complete. By adjusting the drawstring so far as the upper end of the catch piece, the leverage on the bait stick is so slight as to require a mere touch to spring it.

The Ground Snare

For simplicity of construction, few snare traps compare. It is similar to the common snare, and also catches by the feet. This trap consists of three pieces. A catch-piece about three inches long, a bait stick of about six inches, and a stout crotch of proportionate size. Be careful that the bait stick is set *fine* and rests *just beneath* the *tip* of the catch-piece so that a mere touch on the bait will release it.

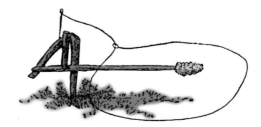

Arrange the noose as in the instance last described, and bait either as therein directed or with an apple or nubbin of corn, as our accompanying cut indicates. Always remembering that the noose should be sufficiently large to insure the bird must step *inside* of it in order to reach the bait.

STEEL TRAPS OF THE MOUNTAIN MEN

The steel trap was the principal device used by trappers, and possessed great advantages over all other traps. It is portable, sets easily and quickly, either on land or beneath the water; can be concealed with ease; secures its victims without injury to their fur, and by the application of the *spring* or *sliding pole* will most often prevent the captive from making his escape by self-amputation, besides placing him beyond the reach of destruction by other animals.

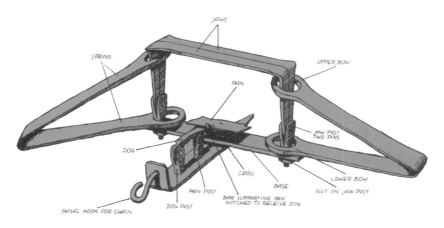

Notes on the Steel Trap

The jaws should not be too thin or sharply cornered. If the jaw is too thin or too sharp, it often severs the animal's leg. At other times the leg is so deeply cut as to easily enable the animal to gnaw or twist it off. This is the common mode of escape with many animals.

The pan should not be too large. This is a very common fault with many steel traps and often defeats its very object. Where the pan is small, when the foot of the animal presses, it will be directly in the center of the snap of the jaw, and he is firmly secured far up on the leg. On the other hand, a large pan nearly filling the space between the jaws as the trap is set may be sprung by a touch on its extreme edge, and the animal's paw is likely to be chopped off altogether by the forcible snap of the jaw.

The springs ought to be strong, tempered, and proportioned. The strength of a perfectly tempered spring will always remain the same, whether in winter or summer, never losing its elasticity.

The jaws should be curved so as to give the bow of the spring a proper sweep to work on. The jaws should lie *flat* when open, and should work easily on their hinges. Each trap should have a strong chain with ring and swivel attached, and the swivel should turn easily.

The true object of the steel trap is to take the animal by the *leg*, thus injuring the skin only in a part where it is valueless.

Never bait a steel trap on the pan. The pan is intended for the *foot* of the game. The bait should be placed as that attention will be *drawn away* from the trap; it being in such a position as will cause the animal to *step on it* when *reaching* for the bait. Following each use, the trap should be thoroughly boiled out, well oiled, and *smoked out* over a fire.

Transportation of Steel Traps

Beaver traps were conveyed west on the rivers and streams, and packaged in pine boxes and barrels, but for ease of conveyance when individual trappers took them into the field they were folded, wrapped in their chains and carried leather bags in canoes and on horse or mule back.

The Spring Pole

This is nearly always used in connection with the steel trap, in the capture of smaller animals. It not only lifts the creature into the air, preventing it from becoming prey to other animals, but it also guards against the escape by the amputation of its leg. This is a very common mode of release with many kinds of game, notably the mink, marten, and muskrat. It is a simple contrivance, i.e. a pole inserted in the ground near the trap. The pole is then bent down, and the trap chain secured to its end. A small, notched peg is next driven into the ground and the top of the pole caught in it, and is thus held in a bent position. When the animal is caught, its struggles release the pole, and the latter, flying up with a jerk, lifts the trap and its occupant into the air, out of the reach of marauders, and beyond the power of escape by self-amputation. Even in the capture of large game, the spring pole often serves a good purpose. A heavy animal's struggles are often so violent as to break even a stout trap or chain; but the force of the spring pole, although insufficient to raise the animal from its feet, often succeeds in easing the strain and saves a trap from being broken to pieces. The power of the pole must of course be proportionate to the weight of the game.

THE SLIDING POLE

The first impulse with almost every aquatic animal when caught in a trap is to plunge headlong into deep water. With the smaller animals, such as the mink and muskrat, this is all that is desired by the trapper, as the weight of the trap with the chain is sufficient to drown its victim. But with larger animals, the beaver and otter for instance, an additional precaution, in the shape of the "sliding pole" is necessary. This consists of a pole about ten feet long, smoothly trimmed of its branches, except at the tip where a few stubs should be left. Insert this end obliquely into the bed of the stream, where the water is deep, and secure the large end to the bank by means of a hooked stick. The ring of the chain should be large enough to slide easily down the entire length of the pole. When the trap is set, the ring should be slipped on the large end of the pole and held in place by resting a stick against it. The animal, when caught, plunges off into deep water and, guided by the pole, is led to the bottom of the river. The ring slides down to the bed of the stream and there holds its catch until drowned.

A trap set for heavy game should never be secured to a stake. Many of the larger and more powerful animals, when caught in a trap secured like this, are apt either to pull or twist their legs off, or break both trap and chain to pieces. To guard against this, the chain should be weighted with a pole or small log of a size proportionate to the dimensions of the game, its weight being merely sufficient to offer a serious encumbrance to the animal without positively checking its movements. This impediment is called the "clog," and is usually attached to the ring of the trap chain by its larger end, the ring being slipped over the latter and secured in place by a wedge.

A *grappling iron* serves the same purpose, and is often used instead. It is attached to the chain by a swivel joint and it offers a serious resistance to the victim who endeavors to run away with it.

The balance pole is very effective. It is simply a long, slender pole fastened in a crotch or tied to the side of a sapling; the trap being secured to the small end. It is balanced so that the weight of the butt will not only lift the trap but the captured animal as well. It is fastened down in the same way as the spring pole and is released by the struggles of the animal.

FUR-BEARING ANIMALS

Note: The foregoing pages of this chapter are largely adapted from the writings of Elmer Harry Kreps, trapper and mountain man.

Beaver

The beaver is an amphibious animal, resembling the muskrat in appearance but much larger. It has the same thick, heavy body, short neck, and scaly tail. The hind feet are large and strong and the toes are webbed; the front feet are small, the tail "paddle shaped," four or five inches wide and about ten inches long. When full grown, the beaver will weigh forty to fifty pounds, although occasionally much larger ones can be found. The under fur is very fine and soft, and is mixed with longer and coarser hairs called "guard hairs." The prevailing color is a rich, reddish brown on the back and sides, and ashy beneath.

The food of the beaver consists mostly of bark, of such woods as poplar, birch, willow, and cottonwood, as well as the roots of the water lily. In the South they also eat corn.

Beavers build houses of sticks, stones, and mud, locating usually in the edge of a pond or lake, but often making a large pond to suit their requirements by building a dam across the stream. Even when their houses are built on a lake or pond, they always build a dam across the outlet, so as to raise the water by two or three feet.

The dams are built of the same material as the houses. Often there are one or two small dams found below the main dam. They are so well made that they will last for many years, and are so tight that the water usually drips evenly over the top.

The houses are also very well made, with walls being several feet in thickness. There are usually two entrances, both being under water. The size and general shape of the house depends on the number of beavers inhabiting it. The house of a full family of beavers will usually measure about twelve feet in diameter at the water line, but will sometimes be even larger. When there are only two or three beavers, the house is much smaller and pointed on the top.

A full family can consist of six to eight members. There are usually two old beavers, two or three two year olds, and two or three young. The reason for this is that the young beavers remain two years with the parents, and as it takes several years for them to grow to their full size, there are always three sizes in a family. When they have reached the age of two years, they start out and make a house of their own, the beavers born the spring before, becoming the medium size, and a new litter taking their place. By autumn, the beavers that have left the main family have their house and dam completed and a store of food laid up for winter.

Many beavers travel about through the summer, following the streams and return to their homes in the early fall. Their food consists of saplings and small trees, which they gnaw off about a foot above the ground, drag into the edge of the water, where they are cut up into pieces of different lengths, stored away, under water in front of the house. The beaver spends the entire winter under the ice. When they feel hungry they will go out and get a piece of wood, take it into their house, eat the bark, and take the peeled stick out again. They repair the house and dam each fall and they also make holes in the bank under water, to which they can retreat in case the house is disturbed or when they hear a noise on the ice.

Trappers who are well acquainted with the habits of the beaver can make a fair estimate of the number of inmates of a house. It sometimes happens that a pair of young beavers—or a lone beaver that has escaped from some family which has been trapped—will locate in an old deserted house. The experienced trapper, however, is not likely to be fooled. He goes along the shore and carefully examines the stumps, where the animals have been cutting trees for food. The amount of wood that has been cut will show, usually; but he has still a better way of determining whether the work was done by one or more beavers. He examines the teeth marks on the stumps and, if they are all alike, he decides that there is not a full family, but only two, or perhaps only one. A lone beaver that has escaped from the trapper is difficult to trap.

In cutting timber, the beaver takes the wood in small chips, gnawing all around the tree, until it falls. He knows absolutely nothing about throwing the tree in the direction in which he wishes it to fall, but lets it fall just as it is inclined to go.

When one finds a family of beavers and expects to trap the same ground each season, he should not attempt to catch them all, as by leaving a few to breed, he is sure of getting beavers each season. The Indians were known to trap only the old beavers, which they did by setting the traps a good distance from the house—for the young beavers never ventured far from home.

Many beavers are trapped in the fall just before the ice forms, but their fur is not prime until mid-winter. In the

166

North they remain in good condition until the first of June; in the South they would probably not be good after the middle of April.

The following methods of trapping are for use in open water, in either the fall or spring. The first method is usually considered best:

Find a place where the bank bluffs a little and the water is of good depth. Make a little pocket in the bank, several inches deep, and set the trap in the water directly in front of this pocket, where the pan of the trap will be about two inches under water. Dip a small stick in whatever scent you are using and fasten it to the bank with a stick, about fourteen inches above the water, and as far back in the pocket as possible. Fasten the trap so that the beaver will drown; the sliding pole is best. Be sure to use a dead pole or stake, as if a green pole is used the other beavers may carry it away, trap and all. This is a very good method for spring and fall, or at any time when there is open water. Here is another method for the same kind of place:

Set the trap under water at the foot of a steep bank and fasten a couple of green poplar or cottonwood sticks on the bank directly over the trap, so that the beaver will step into the trap in trying to reach them. Have the fresh cut ends of the sticks showing plainly, and make your set near the house or dam so that the beavers are sure to see it. Fasten the trap so that the captured animal will be sure to drown. No covering is needed on traps when they are set under water.

Look for the beaver's slides or trails where he drags his food into the water, and if the water is deep enough to drown him, set the trap under about two inches of water, just where he lands on the bank. This set is all right in the fall, when the beaver is laying in his food for the winter, but is not much good in the spring. Some trappers set the trap a foot or more from the shore, where the water is about six inches deep, as by so doing the beaver is caught by the hind foot and is not so likely to escape.

Beavers usually have a slide or trail over the center of the dam, and this makes a very good place to set a trap. Set the trap under water on the upper side of the dam, just where the trail leads over. Be sure to fasten the trap so that the animal will drown, because if it is not drowned, it is almost certain to escape, and even if it does not, the others will be frightened and you will have a hard time getting them.

In the spring, after the ice has gone, it is a good plan to set a few traps along the stream, as the beavers are traveling at this time and you are likely to catch one almost anywhere along the streams. When setting traps in this way, it is best to drench the set with water to remove the human scent. The beaver is seldom afraid of human scent. Beavers may be caught in midwinter and early spring by setting baited traps under the ice. It is not much use to set traps under the ice in early winter, as the beaver's food is still in good condition and they will not take bait well. Moreover, you are likely to frighten them and make them harder to trap later on. The following methods are among the best for use under the ice. The one first given, being most used, is probably the most recommended.

Go close to the beaver's house where the ice is thin, and by cutting small holes in the ice, find a place where the water is about twelve inches deep. Having found such a place, enlarge the hole until it is about sixteen by twenty inches in size, making a pen the same size as the hole, by shoving down dead sticks about four inches apart. If the bottom is very hard, you will have to freeze the sticks to the ice to hold them in place. This may be done by throwing snow in the water and packing it around the sticks and against the edge of the ice. When the pen is completed, cut a piece of green poplar about one and a

168

half or two inches thick and two or three feet long, and fasten it to a stake by one end—the poplar being placed at a right angle to the stake. This green poplar is the bait, and the stake should be driven down in one corner of the pen so that the bait is within two or three inches from the bottom, and close along one side of the pen, extending a foot or more beyond the entrance.

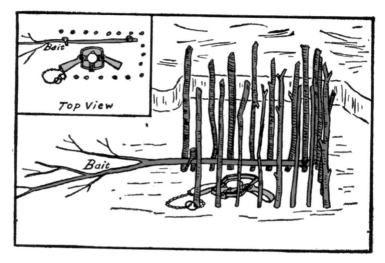

The trap should be staked and set well inside of the pen and quite close to the bait, so that the jaw of the trap will just clear the bait. If the bottom is of thin mud, as is often the case, you will have to make a bed for the trap by sinking a bunch of evergreen boughs inside of the pen. It is also best to fasten the bait near the entrance to prevent the beaver from swinging it around. When the set is completed, cover the hole with evergreen boughs and bank it with snow to keep it from freezing.

It is best to let this set go for about a week before looking at it. The beavers will be frightened and will not approach the set for a few days, but finally one of them will muster up courage to try and pull the bait out of the pen. When he finds it fast, he cuts it off at the entrance of the pen, takes it to the house to eat it; this sharpens his appetite, makes him more courageous, and he finally ventures into the pen for the balance of the bait. In attempting to cut the bait, he places one front foot on the bait and the other one in the trap. When using this set you should use three or four sets at each house. Another good ice method: find the proper depth of water, about fourteen inches, and make a pen of dead sticks arranging them in the form of a half-circle. Now take some green poplar and shove them down firmly into the bottom, about six inches apart, close up to the stakes on the inside of the pen. These bait sticks must be long enough to reach above the ice, so that they will freeze fast at the top. Stake the trap and set it in the center of the enclosure, with the pan about nine inches from the center bait. Throw some snow in the hole, so that it will freeze and hold the bait sticks securely.

The next method is one of the best for use in deep water: Cut a dead pole about four inches in diameter and six or seven feet long. Flatten the pole at one end and loop the trap chain around the pole; then set the trap on the end of the pole and tie it to hold it in place. Now, cut an oblong hole in the ice and place the pole in the water in an inclined position so that the trap is about twelve inches below the ice. Pack wet snow around the pole to hold it in place, fasten two sticks of green poplar in the ice over the trap, one on either side. In attempting to cut the bait, the beaver will put his foot in the trap.

Always fasten your trap to a dead stick or pole, for if a green stake is used, the beavers are likely to carry it away, trap and all. Poplar and cottonwood make the best baits, but in case they cannot be obtained, use birch, willow, or black cherry.

When setting traps near the house, in open water, make as little noise as possible and do not remain in the vicinity longer than necessary.

When trapping in open water, never camp or make a fire near the pond where the beavers are located. In winter, after the ice has formed, it does not matter.

If you find a beaver house in winter when the snow is deep and wish to know if it is inhabited, examine the house, and if the snow is melted on the top, you may be sure there are beavers inside.

Another way to tell whether a house is in use is to cut a hole through the ice and shove down a piece of green poplar, filling the hole with snow. Examine it in about a week, and if the poplar has been cut, you may be sure you have found beavers.

The track of the beaver is seldom seen as they do not move about much in winter and on their trails their tracks are obliterated by the food which they drag into the water. The trapper does not look for tracks, but for more conspicuous signs, such as houses and dams with fresh cut wood.

Mink

This animal has a long, slender body, similar to that of a weasel, to which family it belongs. It inhabits the greater part of North America. The color of its fur varies considerably among individuals, but the general tint is a rich, dark brown. The chin and throat are light colored, sometimes white, sometimes extending down on the throat to a considerable distance. The total length of the animal is from thirteen to sixteen inches. The fur of the mink is excellent in quality.

The mink is an aquatic animal, inhabiting small rivers and streams, and living somewhat like the otter. It has a most wide range of diet, and will eat almost anything that is at all eatable. Fish, frogs, and muskrats are its special delight, and it will occasionally succeed in pouncing upon a snipe or wild duck, which it will greedily devour. Crawfish, snails, and water insects of all kinds are also in its diet, and it sometimes makes a visit to some neighboring poultry yard. A meal of its own offspring sometimes answers the same purpose. The veracity of this animal is its leading characteristic, and it will often run headlong into a naked trap.

The chief occupation of the mink consists in perpetual search for something to eat and, when so engaged, he may be seen running along the bank of the stream, peering into every nook and corner, and literally "leaving no stone unturned" in its eager search. Taking advantage of this habit, it becomes an easy matter to trap the greedy animal. Set your trap in an inch of water near the edge of the stream and directly in front of a steep bank or rock, on which you can place your bait. The bait may be a frog, fish, or head of a bird, suspended about eighteen inches above the water, and should be so situated that in order to reach it, the mink will be obliged to tread upon the trap. The trap may also be set in the water and the bait suspended eighteen inches above it, by the aid of a switch planted in the mud near the trap. It is a good plan to scent the bait with a little honey. If there is deep water near, the sliding pole should be used, and if not, the "spring pole" in order to prevent the captured mink from becoming a prey to larger animals, and also to guard against his escape by amputation, which he would otherwise almost certainly accomplish.

The trap may be set on the land, near the water's edge, baiting as described, and lightly covered with leaves or dirt. Any arrangement of the trap whereby the animal is obliged to tread upon it in order to secure the bait will work.

The trap may also be set at the foot of a tree, and the bait fastened to the trunk, eighteen inches above it. A pen may be constructed and the trap and bait arranged there.

Minks have their regular beaten paths and often visit certain hollow logs in their runways. In these logs they leave unmistakable signs of their presence, and a trap set in such a place will often succeed.

The fur of the mink is in its best condition in the late autumn, winter, and early spring, and the animal should be skinned as you would the fox.

Weasel

The weasel is the smallest of all carnivorous animals. In this country alone, naturalists recognize some twenty species and sub-species, most of which are found in Canada and Alaska, also the Northern and Western states. Of these it is only the Northern varieties, those that become white in winter that is of importance to the trapper. The ermine of Europe is a species of weasel, and the American white weasel is sometimes called the ermine, its fur is used to imitate the fur of that animal.

The change of color in the fur of this animal is not understood by naturalists. It occurs only in the most Northern portions of its range and it is not known whether the animal really sheds its brown summer coat when the cold weather approaches or whether the fur bleaches, but it is certain that the change occurs in some way, the fur becoming white in the fall and changing to brown again in spring.

The smallest variety of the weasel is found in Northwestern Canada and Alaska, where the black tip of the tail so characteristic of the weasel is missing.

The weasel is one of the most blood-thirsty animals and is very courageous. It is a terror to rats, mice, rabbits, partridges, and poultry. It will kill for the love of slaughter, even when not hungry.

Curiosity is highly developed in the weasel. The weasel has a sharp eye and a keen nose, and for their size are very strong, often able to move a fair sized rabbit.

For trapping this animal the No. 1 ½ trap is recommended, and many trappers prefer a trap that is loosely hinged and springs easily. Any trap will hold a weasel but, when caught in the smaller sizes, they quite often double up about the jaws and when they die and freeze in that position it is difficult to remove them from the trap. As the animal is so very light in weight, it is necessary that the trap springs very easily.

One method of setting is to place the trap inside of a small enclosure with chunks of wood, bark, sticks, or whatever is most convenient. No covering is needed but when setting on the snow, make a bed of evergreen boughs for the trap to rest on. Rotten wood will answer just as well. Fasten the bait with a stick just back of the trap so that the weasel will be obliged to stand on the trap when attempting to remove the bait, for it should be remembered that they will never eat any food where they find it if able to move it away. Fasten the trap securely for some larger animal is likely to be caught. Do not place the traps far apart, where tracks are seen in fair numbers, and drag a fresh killed rabbit from set to set, splitting it open with a knife so as to leave a bloody trail. Any weasel that strikes the trail is sure to follow it.

For bait, rabbit is preferred to anything else, as it contains more blood than other baits and fresh blood is the best possible scent to attract the weasel.

The tracks of the weasel resemble those of the mink but are considerably smaller. The average length of jump is perhaps about eighteen inches.

Marten

The marten is a carnivorous animal belonging to the same family as the weasel. The pine marten is found throughout

the timbered regions of Canada and Alaska, also in the
mountainous districts of the Western states.

In size the marten is about the same as the mink of the
North and East, being somewhat lighter in the body, but the
longer fur causes it to appear fully as large. It has longer legs
than the mink, and the feet are larger and heavily furred. The
tail is thick and bushy, the ears and eyes are large, and the
muzzle is more pointed than that of the mink. The fur is very
fine and soft, the color varying from a rich yellow to almost
black. The fur of the tail is darker than that of the body, and the
face lighter. The ears, on the edges, are grayish white and there
is always a yellow or orange spot on the throat.

In the more Southern portions of their range, the martens
are quite pale. The finest and darkest skins come from
Labrador and the country East and South of Hudson Bay, also
from Northern British Columbia and the interior of Alaska
and the Yukon province. The marten is strictly an animal of
the woods, being found only in the heavily timbered country.
Their favorite haunts are in the rough, broken country, where
the timber is of various kinds. They feed on rabbits, squirrels,
mice, birds, and eggs, and probably have no trouble in
obtaining a sufficient amount of food. But unlike the mink
and the weasel, they never kill more than is needed to supply
their wants.

The young are usually born in April, and there are from
three to five at a birth. One peculiarity regarding the martens
is the fact that they occasionally disappear from a locality
in which they were formerly numerous. The common
supposition is that they migrate to new feeding grounds when
food becomes scarce.

The marten travels mostly in the gullies and depressions
on the mountains and hills. As they usually follow the same
route, when one sees their tracks in such a place, he can be
reasonably sure, if he sets his trap there, that he will make a
catch. They are not shy or suspicious and are easily caught.
In many ways, marten trapping is the most pleasant as well
as the most profitable kind of trapping. As they are found
only in the timbered country, the trapper does not feel the
storms like he would in an open country. They are easily

caught, light to carry, and easily skinned. Moreover, they are a very valuable fur and if one is in a good locality, he will make a large catch in a season. They usually become prime for trapping around mid-October and remain in good condition until the last of March.

In countries where the snow is not too deep, the traps are set in small enclosures, the same as for the mink.

If there is snow on the ground, set the traps as follows. With your snowshoes, tramp the snow down solid at the foot of a tree and build a small pen of stakes or chunks split from an old stump. The stakes or chunks are arranged so as to form the sides of the pen, and the sides are placed about six or seven inches apart, the tree forming the back of the pen. Then roof the pen with evergreen boughs to protect the trap from the falling snow. It is a good idea to leave a couple of boughs hanging down over the mouth of the pen so as to hide the bait from the birds and also to prevent the rabbits from entering the pen. Set the trap on a bed of boughs just inside of the pen, and cover lightly with tips of evergreen. The bait is placed on a stick behind the trap. Fasten the trap to a toggle, but if only marten is expected, the trap may be fastened in almost any way, as they seldom escape. It is also a good idea to bend a small twig and place it under the pan of the trap to prevent it from being sprung by birds, squirrels, and weasels.

For bait, rabbit, partridge, squirrel, fish, small birds, or meat of almost any kind is acceptable; the majority prefer to use fresh bait. Some trappers advise dragging a piece of fresh,

bloody meat along the line to lead the marten to the trap.

Another very good method is the following: Find a small spruce, about three inches in diameter, and cut the tree about two feet above the snow, leaving the top of the stump V shape. Draw the tree forward and lay it over the stump, so that the butt of the tree will be three or three and a half feet above the snow. Now, about a foot back from the end, flatten off a place for the trap and set the trap on the pole. Tie the trap fast with a light string and loop the chain around the tree. Split the butt of the tree and fasten the bait in the split. This is a very good set, possessing advantages over most methods. The birds cannot eat the bait, the trap is not bothered by weasels or rabbits, the marten must stand on the trap when trying to get the bait, and when caught, falls off the pole and cannot get back.

In the mountains, where the snow falls deep, the traps are set on the trees, five or six feet above the snow. The most common way is to make two cuts in the tree with an axe and drive in two wooden pegs, about five inches apart. Set the trap and place it on the pegs, one peg passing through the bow of the spring, the other between the jaws and the bottom of the trap. Draw the chain around the tree and staple solidly. The bait is pinned to the tree, about a foot above the trap. A bunch of boughs may be placed over the bait to hide it from birds.

If desired, a notch may be cut in the tree and a trap set in the notch. The notch should be about four inches deep and about twelve inches from top to bottom. Cut the bottom smooth, so the trap will set solid and fasten the bait in the top of the notch. Staple the trap to the tree. If desired, you can lean a pole against the tree for the marten to run up on, but this is not necessary.

The canny trapper is always on the lookout for places in which the trap may be set without much labor. Sometimes a tree can be found with a hollow in one side and this makes a good place for a set. Lean a pole against the tree, with one end resting in the hollow, set a trap on the pole and place bait in the cavity above the trap. At other times a cavity may be made in the side of a rotten stub and a trap set in the same way. The track of the marten resembles that of the mink, except that it is a trifle larger and the footprint wider in proportion to the length. The toes do not make as clear a print as do those of the mink, the feet being more heavily furred.

Otter

The otter is a carnivorous animal, somewhat resembling the mink in appearance. They are found in various parts of the world and will be met with in most of the wilder parts of North America. The Northern or Canadian otter is the most common, but there are other varieties known as the Carolina otter, the Florida otter, and the Newfoundland otter. In habits and general appearance they are all similar.

A distinct species is found in the North Pacific, and is known as the sea otter. This animal is considerably larger than the fresh water species, and has a shorter tail. The fur is of great value.

The otter is an aquatic animal, living in and near the streams and lakes and getting its living from them. It has a long body, short, stout legs, and webbed feet; the tail is long, thick at the base, and tapering to a point. The neck is thick, the head comparatively small, with small ears, set well down on the sides of the head. The fur is of two kinds: the under fur being fine, soft and wavy, and of a light silvery color; while the outer fur or guard hairs, are longer, coarser, and usually straight, the color varying from brown to almost black. The fur of the tail and under parts is shorter and stiffer than that on the back, sides, and neck; that on the under parts having a silvery tint.

Otters frequently measure three and one-half feet in length and weigh from fifteen to twenty-five pounds. The skin, when stretched, will often measure five feet from tip to tip, and sometimes even more.

The food of the otter consists principally of fish, trout being their favorite food; but they also feed on muskrats, clams, frogs, and the smaller animal life, found in the beds of streams and lakes.

They capture muskrats by entering their houses and their holes in the banks. Otters usually make burrows in the banks of streams, lining the nest with leaves and grass. The entrances to these burrows are under the water. The young are born in April and May and there are from two to four in a litter.

The otter is a great traveler, following the lakes and waterways, sometimes going a distance of one hundred miles on a single trip. Apparently he is always in a great hurry to reach a certain place—some lake or pond—at which, having reached, he may remain for several months, and then again he may leave immediately after his arrival.

Otters sometimes have slides on the banks of streams, down which they slide into the water, apparently as a pastime. They also have landing places on the banks of streams and on logs projecting into the water, where they go to roll in the grass and leaves, or to lie in the sun. These places are seldom visited in the fall, but in the spring, they will land at almost every place as they come along.

In traveling, they usually follow the center of the stream, as they are more at home in the water than on land. In winter they travel under the ice, wherever the water is deep enough to allow them passage. The otter's legs being very short, it has a peculiar method of traveling on the ice or snow. It throws himself forward, sliding on its belly, and by repeating the move in rapid succession, is enabled to get along at a surprising rate of speed.

Wherever there is a sharp bend in the stream, the otter will make a short cut across the point, and if the stream is traveled much, you will find a well-defined trail in such a place. Where two streams lie close together, they sometimes have a trail from one stream to another. Also wherever a long point of land

180

projects into a lake, they are likely to have a trail across the point.

The otter appears to be on very friendly terms with the beaver, and if there are any beavers in the country, the otter is sure to find them and will spend considerable time in the same pond. When there are a number of families of beavers in the same locality, the otter will spend nearly all of its time with the beavers, visiting from one family to another. Wherever he finds beaver cutting along the stream, he examines it, and will most likely follow up the stream to find the beaver.

In the North, the otter becomes prime about the first week in November, and remains in good condition until about the first of June. In the South they are seldom prime until the first of December, and commence to shed from the first to the fifteenth of April. The fur of the otter is valuable; the dark, straight haired ones being worth the most. The most valuable otters come from the far North, but they are probably more plentiful in the South, and the Southern trapper has the advantage of having open water all winter.

The great point to keep in mind when trapping for otter is that they are very shy of the scent of man; more so perhaps than any other animal. And unless great care is observed, they are likely to be frightened entirely out of the locality in which you are trapping. This human scent theory is disputed by some trappers. But if one will use a little judgment, he will readily understand why human scent is alarming to many wild animals. Man is the natural enemy of all wild animal life, and all wild creatures realize this fact. Any indication of the presence of man puts the animal on guard; this is especially the case in the wilderness where the animals are not accustomed to seeing the tracks of man. When an animal finds human scent, he has positive proof that man has been in that vicinity.

If there is no scent, footprints and other human signs are not so alarming, as they are likely to be mistaken for signs made by some wild animal.

Remember, the otter is sure to visit the beavers, if there are any about, so if you know of a family of beavers, go to that place and if you can find an old beaver dam on the stream somewhere, below where the beavers are located, make a break in the center of this dam, so that all of the water will flow through this opening and set the trap in the water, in the upper end of this passage. Narrow down the passage to about eight inches by driving a few old stakes on each side of the trap. The trap may be staked, but it is better if the water is deep enough to use a sliding pole, so that the captured animal will drown. No covering is needed on the trap but, after it is set, the entire setting should be drenched with water to remove the human scent. This is an excellent set and will remain in working order until late in the fall, as the water immediately above the break in the dam will not freeze until long after other water is closed by ice. Even in the coldest weather this set may be kept from freezing by roofing it over with evergreen boughs and banking it well with snow.

Beavers and beaver dams are not found in every locality, but wherever otters are found traveling on small streams, they may be trapped in the following manner:

Find a narrow place in the stream where the water flows smoothly and narrow up the stream by placing a bunch of old dead brush in each side, leaving a passage of about eight inches in the middle. Lay a few stones among the brush to keep them in place. Set the trap in the opening and splash water over the brush and banks. The trap may be staked, but it is better to fasten to a clog. Cut a small sapling of such a size that the ring of the chain will just pass over the butt of the sapling. Slip the ring over the clog and fasten it by splitting the butt and drive a wedge in the split, or by driving a staple over the ring. The clog may be placed on the upper side of the brush, used to block the stream, and the top may be tied to the shore, so that it will not be carried away by high water. In very small streams, a narrow passage may be made by simply placing a few stones in either side, leaving a narrow passage in the middle, in which to set the trap.

When you can find a sharp bend in the stream with a trail across the point, set the trap in the water at the end of the trail. Use same care as advised for the other sets.

For spring trapping this method is excellent: if you can find one of the otter's landing places on the bank, prepare the place for setting in the fall in the following manner. Make a nest for

182

the trap in the center of the trail and fill the nest with grass and leaves. Lay a bunch of dead brush or a chunk of rotten wood on each side of the trail, so as to leave only a narrow passage and cut a clog and lay it in place. The otters seldom visit these places in the fall, so there is no danger of frightening them. In the spring, before the snow is all gone, go and set your trap in the prepared place, covering it with the leaves and grass and attach to the clog, covering the entire setting with a little snow. As the snow melts, it takes with it all of the scent and signs, leaving the trap ready for the first otter that comes along.

If you do not find the landing places until after the snow is gone, set the traps just the same, washing the scent away by sprinkling with water or set the traps in the water where the otter climbs up the bank.

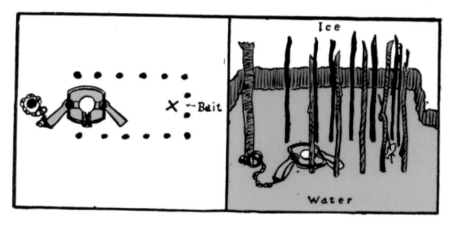

One of the best methods of trapping an otter in winter, after the streams are closed with ice, is as follows: Find a long pool of still water where you are sure the otter will be traveling under the ice, and at either end of this pool, where the water is about ten inches deep. Cut a hole through the ice, make a pen of dead sticks in the water, making the pen about nine inches wide, by twelve or fifteen inches deep. Now take a fish and fasten it to a stick in the back of the pen, and set the trap in the entrance, staking it securely. Drive the stake about ten inches in front of the pen and directly in front of the trap. The object in this is to cause the otter, in entering, to twist his body, in which act, he will put his foot down in the trap. Throw some

183

snow in the hole so it will freeze over. The bait should be renewed once a week. In case you cannot get fish for bait, use the head of a rabbit, the breast of a partridge, or a piece of muskrat. The bait should be skinned.

If the ice has formed when the water was above its usual level, there will be an air space between the water and the ice. In such a case, cut a hole through the ice at the edge of the water, placing a piece of beaver castor on a stick behind the trap. The hole may be closed by covering with a block of ice.

When the otter has been working on a lake for some time, you will find it coming out at the spring holes, which are found on nearly all lakes. In such places the water is always shallow, and a trap may be set on the bottom directly under the hole. Great care must be used however, for if the otter is not caught the first time it comes out, as they will be frightened away.

Otters often land on the logs which project into the water. When you can find such a log, cut a notch for a trap, so that it will set about two inches deep, and place some mud in the notch so as to hide the fresh cutting. Some very successful trappers set their traps in this way, and place some good scent on the log above the trap.

If you can find an otter slide, find the place where the animal lands on the bank to visit the slide and set the trap under about two inches of water. The trap should be set at the foot of the slide, so as to catch the animal by the breast or body.

Otters often travel in pairs, and it is usually advisable to set two or three traps on one stream.

Do not make your camp near the stream, and do not travel along the stream more than necessary. In looking at the traps, do not go too close, unless the traps need your attention.

There is no way in which the sea otter can be trapped and they are hunted only with rifles. The methods employed in hunting them have been very successful and as a consequence the animal has been practically exterminated.

The track of the otter is peculiar, owing to their strange mode of travel. Their method of travel is a series of plunging slides and in the snow they make a deep furrow, their footprints being from four to eight feet apart, according to the "sliding conditions." When two or more are traveling in company, they will usually all run in the same trail. Their tracks are as a rule, only seen on lakes and streams, but occasionally they will go overland from one stream to another. The footprints will measure about one and one-half or one and three-fourths inches in length and about the same in width.

Wolverine

Perhaps the rarest of all the fur bearing animals, as well as the least known, is the wolverine. This animal belongs to the marten family and is the largest, strongest, and most cunning of the genus. In fact, it's claimed to be the most cunning and wary of all the furbearing animals, and among the trappers has an unenviable reputation.

It is strictly a Northern animal and is found scattered over the greater portion of Canada and Alaska, ranging Southward into the most Northern portion of the United States. In the Rocky mountain region it is found as far south as Wyoming. They are not plentiful anywhere and are probably found in the greatest numbers in the Alaskan interior, Yukon, Mackenzie, and Northern British Columbia.

While the wolverine is classed among the martens, it appears to be the connecting link between martens and bears for it is stoutly built and very bear-like in general appearance, walking on the soles of its feet. An average specimen will measure about thirty inches from the end of the nose to the base of the tail. The tail is about ten inches in length, exclusive of the long hair and is very stumpy and bushy. The fur is long and flowing and is fairly fine. The general color is a dull brown with black legs and feet and a black patch about the eyes. A spot or stripe of lighter color sweeps along the sides. The teeth are large and strong and the curved claws are white, contrasting sharply with the black fur of the feet and legs.

The wolverine makes its home in a burrow. Naturalists disagree as to the number of young and the time of birth. Some claim that the young animals are born in May, while some put the time as late as December. As the other members of the marten family give birth to their young in April and May, it is safe to assume that the young of the wolverine are born about the same time, and that the number would be from three to five in a litter.

The animal is a great traveler, straying sometimes thirty miles in each direction from its home. It is not a rapid traveler, however, and it is claimed that a man can easily outrun it.

The wolverine is also known under other fancy names, the most common of which is "carcajou." In Europe it is called the "glutton" from its supposed voracious appetite. Among the Indians of the Northwest it is known as the "mountain devil," and in British Columbia is sometimes called the "skunk bear."

The animal really does bear some resemblance to the skunk in its appearance and actions, the most noticeable of which is its habits of raising its tail when disturbed or when it stops to listen to noise. Sometimes it will stand on its hind legs in order to get a better view of some object that has aroused its interest.

The wolverine is not as active as the other members of the genus, but its strength and cunning fully compensate for all that it lacks in activity. It can seldom capture enough game to satisfy its hunger; therefore it seeks out and robs the catches of other animals, also robbing the traps of their bait and the captured animals. For this reason the animal is despised and dreaded by the trapper. Once one has found the trap line it will follow the trail to the end, destroying the sets and eating the baits and catch. What it cannot eat, it will carry away and conceal presumably for a future meal. It will also sometimes enter the trapper's cabin and destroy or defile all that it cannot eat.

Many strange stories are told of the animal's cunning and evil ways. While some of these tales are no doubt true, it's safe to say that the majority have no foundation whatever. There is no doubt that the wolverine is exceedingly wary and that it is a great mischief maker.

Not being plentiful in any one locality the animals are seldom trapped and what few are caught are taken when they are visiting camps or while robbing the traps of the bait and catch. Trapping them at all times is difficult work, owing to the natural wariness of the animal. That the trap must be well concealed and that the animal must be taken when off its guard goes without saying. The No. 4 trap should be used and only those which have strong springs, as the wolverine possesses great strength.

These animals are not sought by the trapper and he may consider himself lucky if there are none of them on his trapping ground. When they are found, the trapper's aim is to get rid of them and the most certain way appears to be by means of poison.

Muskrat

The muskrat is a small herbivorous animal of the amphibious class. Its head and body are from thirteen to fifteen inches in length. The tail is nine or ten inches, two edged, and for two-thirds its length is rudder shaped and covered with scales and thin, short hair. The front feet are small, the hind feet, large and slightly webbed, making the animal an expert swimmer. The color of the fur is brown above and ashy beneath.

The muskrat is a nocturnal animal, but is sometimes seen in the daytime. Their food consists of grass and roots, fruit, grains, and vegetables. They will also eat clams, sometimes, when food is scarce. They thrive best in sluggish streams and ponds, bordered with grass. Their houses are dome shaped and rise sometimes to a height of five feet from the water. The entrances are at the bottom, under water, so that the inside of the house is not exposed to the open air. From six to ten muskrats are sometimes found in one house.

The muskrats found on streams do not build houses, but live in holes in the bank, the entrances of which are also under water. The muskrat is found throughout the greater part of the United States and Canada. Muskrats are most plentiful in some parts of Western Canada. These animals are very prolific, bringing forth from six to nine at a birth and three litters in a season. They have many enemies, such as the fox, mink, otter and owl, but their greatest enemy is man.

Muskrats are trapped in the fall, winter, and spring, but they are not prime until mid-winter, and some are not fully prime until the first of March. Nevertheless, they are more easily caught in the fall, and as the skins bring a fair price, the most trapping is done at this time, which is for "bank rats," those living in holes in the banks. Where the muskrats live in houses, they are trapped mostly after the ice had formed.

In the far North the skins are in good condition until the first of June, while in the extreme South they should not be trapped after the first of April. The muskrats found in settled districts are larger and better furred than those of the wilderness. Also, those found east of the Mississippi River are larger than those of the West.

When trapping for these animals, the traps should always be staked full length of chain into deep water, so that the captured animal will drown, as otherwise they are almost certain to twist off the foot and escape, unless they are caught by a hind foot. Many trappers set their traps several inches under water, as by so doing they catch the rat by a hind foot and there is very little danger of them escaping. Some stake their traps the length of the chain into deep water and drive another stake about a foot beyond. The muskrat, when caught, winds the chain around the outer stake and is thus prevented from reaching the bank. Others prefer to tie a stone on the end of the chain and lay the stone in deep water.

One of the most common methods of trapping the muskrat is to find their slides on the bank and set the trap at the foot of the slide under about two and a half or three inches of water. No covering is needed.

If you can find a log with one end lying in the water, examine it, and if there are muskrat droppings on the log, cut a notch for the trap, so that it will be just under water when set in the notch. The chain may be stapled to the log.

Another good way is to find their holes in the bank and set a trap in the entrance, staking into deep water.

If the water is still and there is much grass in the water, look around, and you will find their feeding beds—ones of grass which appear to be floating on the water. Set traps on these beds, under water.

If you know there are muskrats about and you cannot find any of the places described above, select a steep bank and set the trap under two or three inches of water at the foot of the bank. Pin a piece of bait to the bank about ten inches above the trap. To trap muskrats in their houses in winter, cut a hole in the side of the house and set the trap inside, on the bed. Fasten the trap to a stick outside of the house and close the opening tight, so the diving hole will not freeze. The traps should be visited in the evening and morning.

In the spring, when the ice has just commenced to melt, you will find small piles of grass roots projecting above the ice. Move this aside and you will find a hole in the ice, with a feed bed directly in under it. Set a trap on this bed and cover the hole.

The best baits for muskrats are sweet apple, parsnip, carrot, pumpkin, corn, and the flesh of the muskrat. While they do not eat the meat, they will go to smell at it, which is all that is needed. Muskrat musk, beaver castor, and catnip are all attractive to the muskrat.

Raccoon

The raccoon is allied to the bear family. It is found only on the Western Continent, where it is represented by two species: the common raccoon of the United States and the crab-eating raccoon of the tropics. The common raccoon, called coon by hunters and trappers, is found throughout the Mississippi Valley and all of the states East and also in the Pacific Coast states, Western British Columbia, Lower Ontario, New Brunswick, and Nova Scotia. They are found in greatest numbers in those states bordering on the Gulf of Mexico.

The common raccoon is the one of principal interest to the trapper and fur dealer. The body is short and stout, like that of the badger. Its head resembles that of the fox. Its tail is ten or twelve inches long, thick and bushy. The feet are bare and the toes long. The general color is grey, the tips of the hairs being darker. Occasionally a very dark one is found, in some cases being almost black. The tail is ringed with black and a black band crosses the eyes. The raccoon is a nocturnal animal, is omnivorous and hibernates during cold weather, coming out in search of food only on warm nights.

Their food consists of green corn, grapes and other fruits, fish, frogs, clams, birds and their eggs and they are also fond of poultry. In search of food, they travel mostly along the streams and in early fall, in the corn fields.

They den in hollow trees, having an entrance at a considerable distance from the ground. In mountainous districts, they also den in holes among the rocks.

The young are born in April and May and from two to six are brought forth at a time. Their mating season is generally about the last of February and the beginning of March, and at this time the males travel considerably, crawling into a hollow tree wherever daylight overtakes them.

In the North they become prime about November 1st; the season being later in the South. They remain in good condition until late in the spring. The fur is used mostly for coats and robes.

The nature and habits of the raccoon, like all other animals, differs considerably from location to location. In most sections they are very easily trapped, but those found in some parts of the Pacific Coast are said to be quite cunning. Any of the articles of food mentioned above, will make good bait; fresh fish however, being preferred. The traps to use are the No. 1 1/2 Newhouse or Hawley & Norton, the No. 2 Victor, and the Nos. 2 and 3 Oneida Jump and Blake & Lamb traps. The trap should be fastened to a clog, and in some cases an iron drag could be used to advantage, as the coon will get fastened up on the first brush he comes to.

The most common method is to set the trap in the entrance of a pen of stakes, at the edge of the water where the animals travel. The trap may be set dry or under water, as preferred, and the bait should be placed in the back of the pen.

Another very good method, much used in the South, is to fasten a piece of bright tin or a piece of a white dish, on the pan of the trap and set the trap under about two inches of water, near the bank. No bait is used, but a little scent may be used on the bank to good advantage.

The Southern Trappers sometimes find a tree, stump or rock in the edge of the water, and set the trap in the water, just where the coon will walk, when passing around the obstruction. A fence made of brush will answer the same purpose.

Where the bank is steep and the water is shallow, dig a six-inch hole, straight into the bank at the edge of the water. Fasten some bait in the back of the hole and set the trap in the water, directly in front of the hole.

If you find a log lying across the stream and there are signs of coons about, cut a notch in the top of the log and set the trap in the notch, covering with rotten wood or moss. You are also likely to catch a fox in a set of this kind.

When a den tree can be found, cut a pole five or six feet long and six inches thick; lean it against the tree and set the trap on the pole. Cover the trap lightly with moss and staple to the tree.

Any natural enclosure along a stream, such as a hollow log or a hole under a stump, makes a good place to set a trap. When trapping for foxes with water sets, many coons will be caught in the traps.

One of the best scents for coon is made as follows: To a pint of fish oil, add twenty or thirty drops of oil of anise and two ounces of strained honey. Pure fish oil is used by some trappers and beaver castor, muskrat musk and oil of anise are also good.

The trail of the raccoon is somewhat like that of the mink, but the tracks are larger. The animal makes the print of the entire foot and the long slender toes show plainly. The print of the hind foot will be from two and a quarter to three inches in length.

Badger

Badgers are burrowing, carnivorous animals. They are found in North America and various parts of the Old World; one species being found in Europe, one in India and another in Japan. There are several varieties of the American species and they are found at present only west of the Mississippi River, although formerly they ranged as far east as Ohio. They are perhaps most numerous on the High, dry plains just east of the Rocky Mountains, and range from Mexico to well up into Canada. They were at one time quite numerous in Wisconsin and Minnesota, as well as others of the Northern and Central States, but today are found but rarely in those sections. Wisconsin is sometimes called the "Badger State" because of the numbers of these animals found there by the early settlers. The badger is an animal of peculiar build, having a heavy, broad body, at times appearing almost flat, as when it crouches close to the ground, and the legs are short and stout. The feet are furnished with long, strong claws, adapted for digging. The tail is short, the ears short and round, the eyes small and black. A full grown specimen will measure about two feet or more from the end of the nose to the base of the tail.

The color is a grizzly, yellowish grey, being darker on the back. A white line traverses the face, head and neck, bordered with black, which latter marking extends around the eyes. The sides of the face and the throat are white, and there is a black patch in front of each ear. The legs and feet are black. The back and sides of the body are mottled somewhat by narrow streaks of darker fur.

The fur, or more properly speaking, the hair, is long and appears to be parted on the back as it hangs off to either side from a line down the center of the back. Each separate hair shows a number of colors and it is this that gives the animal the peculiar grizzled appearance. Although the animal is of a heavy build, the casual observer would scarcely credit the animal with the great strength which it really possesses, because of the apparently soft and flabby body. However, the strength of the animal is surprising. They are slow moving creatures and were it not for their strength and powers of digging, they would have difficulty in procuring a sufficient amount of food.

They feed on the small burrowing animals mainly, such as the prairie dog, the gopher, and the pouched rat, and they are enabled to capture many of these animals by digging them out of the dens. They also eat mice and reptiles and the eggs and young of ground-nesting birds.

Being such an expert digger, the badger makes a deep den. The entrance to the den is wide and surrounded by a mound of earth. In addition to the main den the animal has a number of others nearby, so that one would scarcely know which of them is the main burrow. They are hibernating animals and remain in the dens during the cold portion of the winter.

The animal is of a rather timid nature, and when alarmed seeks safety in the den if possible, but when surprised far from the den, will hide wherever possible and failing to find cover will flatten down close to the ground and by remaining very quiet, will try to escape notice. However when pursued, and finding escape impossible, they will fight desperately.

The young are born in early spring, there being as a rule three or four in a litter. The fur of the badger is used for making brushes of various kinds, its peculiar texture making it especially desirable for this purpose. It is not used for wearing apparel. The No. 3 trap is the proper size to use for this animal, and only the stronger ones should be used. They are caught and held occasionally in smaller and weaker traps, yet such cases are exceptions.

As the animal is not a valuable one and is not found in large numbers in any one locality, they are not much sought by the trappers and the most of the Skins which reach the market are from the animals caught in traps set for other game. The wolf and coyote trappers catch them occasionally, as they may be captured by any of the methods used for those animals.

Perhaps the best way in which to capture the badger is to set the trap at the entrance to the main burrow, that is, the one showing the most use. The trap should be set just outside of the entrance and should be securely staked, using a long stake driven out of sight in the ground. The jaws of the trap should be parallel with the passage, so that the badger will step between the jaws, and not over them. It should be bedded down so that the covering will match with the surroundings.

Traps may also be set with bait. On the plains, material for enclosures can not be found but the traps may be set between clumps of sage brush or cactus, placing the bait behind the trap, the setting being so arranged that the badger will be obliged to walk over the trap in order to reach the bait. The trap should be securely staked in all cases. For bait, rabbit, sage hen, prairie dog or almost any kind of fresh meat may be used.

Fox

The various members of the fox family are found in almost all parts of the world but are most abundant in the Northern Hemisphere. There are many species and varieties, but it is those of North America that are of the most interest to the trapper. Those found on this continent are the red, the gray, the kit and Arctic foxes, and there are a number of varieties of the red and gray species. The black, silver and cross foxes are supposed to be only color varieties of the red, but why this occurs, and only in the North, is a mystery.

The silver or black fox is the most beautiful and most valuable of all the foxes. It is found in the high, northern latitudes of both continents. In this country, it is found as far south as the northern tier of states. They are most abundant in the interior of Alaska, the Northwest Territories, Ontario, Northern Quebec, Labrador, and Newfoundland. The red fox is the most common and is distributed over a larger territory than the other varieties. They range from the northern timber-line, to well down in the Southern States. They are probably most abundant in the Eastern provinces of Canada and the England States, but they are found in fair numbers in parts of New York, Pennsylvania, West Virginia, Tennessee, Arkansas, Missouri, Michigan, and the larger part of Canada and Alaska.

The Gray fox is one of the least valuable, and is most abundant in the Southern States. In the East they range as far north as Connecticut. In some places they have supplanted the Red species, and in other places the grays have disappeared and the reds have taken their place.

The fox, as well as the wolf and coyote, belongs to the dog family. The different species are all practically the same size, but the same varieties vary in size in different localities. The average weight is from nine to ten pounds. In general appearance they somewhat resemble the dog, being rather light of build, considering their height. The ears are erect and pointed, the tail thick and bushy, and the muzzle small and pointed. The fur varies in the different species, being coarse and rather short on the gray, while that of the Silver fox is extremely fine and soft.

The mating season comes in February, and the young are born usually in April, there being from four to nine in a litter. They make dens in the sand hills and in rocky districts, den in the rocks. Except during the breeding season they spend very little time in the dens, but lie during the day in some clump of brush or weeds, or often on top of a stump or log. In mountainous sections they lie during the day, somewhere on the mountainside and come down into the valleys at night in search of food.

The fox is not strictly a carnivorous animal. When food is scarce they often feed on apples and other fruits, but their regular food is flesh. They are fond of partridge, rabbits, mice, skunk, muskrat or opossum flesh, carrion of almost all kinds, fish, eggs, poultry, and often they come around the camps and gather up the scraps, bread, bacon rinds etc. If they are given time and not disturbed they become quite bold in coming to such places for food and the trappers sometime take advantage of this peculiarity by baiting them awhile before setting the trap.

The fox in the North becomes prime in the beginning of November and remains in good condition until the middle of March, when the fur begins to take on a rubbed and woolly appearance. In the South they do not become prime until the last of November or the beginning of December and go out of prime in February. Most of the foxes are trapped in the fall before the ground freezes too hard for dry sets, and of course, many of them are not prime.

In places where there are springs and small streams, there is no better method than the old water set, which is made as follows: It is best to find a spring which does not freeze, but for early fall trapping a brook will do. The rise and fall of the water in small streams sometimes makes trouble, and a spring or small pond gives best results. The spring should be at least four feet in diameter and should be prepared for the set in the summer, but if care is used, may be fixed up during the trapping season. A moss covered stone or a sod (according to surroundings) should be placed about a foot and a half from shore, and should rise about two or three inches above the water. This is the bait sod. The trap is set half way between the sod and the shore, and the jaws, springs and chain should be covered with mud, or whatever is found in the bottom of the spring.

The pan of the trap should just be covered with water. Now take a nice piece of moss or sod and place it on the pan of the trap, so that it will rise an inch above the water. When properly placed, this sod will look natural and will, apparently be a safe stepping place for the fox. The pan should be so adjusted that

it will not spring too easily. A small piece of bait and also some scent should be placed on the larger sod.

In making this set you should wade up the outlet of the spring, and stand in the water while making the set. Do not touch the bank or any of the surroundings. The trap should be fitted with a chain about three feet in length, with a two prong drag attached, but most trappers simply wire a stone of eight or ten pounds weight to the end of the chain. The drag, whatever is used, should be buried in the bed of the spring.

Many trappers recommend the flesh of the muskrat, skunk, opossum or house-cat for bait, and it should be allowed to taint by remaining about a week in a glass jar. This method was first used by William Schofield a famous fox trapper of the Eastern states. Two men have been known to catch over one hundred foxes in a season with this method, besides considerable other furs taken in the same traps, for the method is good for many other animals besides the fox.

One trapper recommends setting the trap in exactly the same manner, except that the bait sod is omitted, and the bait, a bird, is fastened by means of a stick thrust in the bottom of the spring. The stick must be entirely out of sight, and the bird, apparently, floating in the water. Both of these methods are very good, and are especially recommended for the novice, as they are the easiest and surest methods to start on. The water sets given above, can of course, only be used in certain places, for in some of the best fox countries, springs cannot be found, and even the streams are not suitable for trapping. For this reason many professional fox trappers prefer to use dry land sets, and the blind set will be found to be one of the very best.

Look for fox tracks in old stock trails, foot paths, old roads in the woods, openings under fences, etc., and having first cleaned the traps by boiling or washing, find a narrow place in the trail and dig out a nest for the trap. Make this nest so that when the trap is set in it, the jaws will lie lengthwise of the trail. Line this nest with dry grass or leaves, and having attached the trap to some sort of a drag, set it and place it in the place prepared. Fill in all around the outside of the jaws with dry dirt, and cover the springs. Now lay a piece of clean paper over the trap and cover all with about one-fourth inch of dirt, making it look like the other parts of the trail as much as possible. The chain and drag must be carefully concealed.

It is best to have a basket or piece of canvas in which to place the dirt while making the set and to carry away what is not needed. Do not spit near the trap, and do not leave any signs of your presence. It is not necessary to wear gloves, but the hands should be kept clean. This is an excellent method, especially for the old, sly animals.

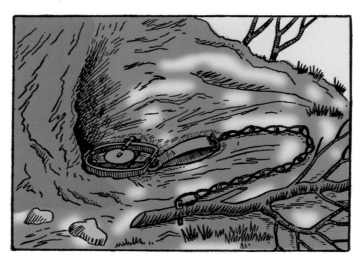

The professional trappers of the East use the bait method, mostly, and although the different trappers use different baits and scents, the methods of setting the traps are all, practically the same.

Prepare your bait about a week before you want to set the traps, by cutting into pieces about half the size of an egg, and placing in a clean jar to become tainted. Put a little bit of scent on each bait before placing in jar. There are different ways for preparing the traps; most trappers prefer to boil them in hemlock boughs, or lay them over night in running water. Wear clean gloves when handling the traps and carry them in a clean basket. Now find an old stump or a rock along some hillside, and dig a hole under it making the hole four or five inches in diameter and ten or twelve inches deep. Stake the trap solid, driving stake out of sight, and set the trap about ten inches in front of the hole. Cover the trap first with a piece of clean paper and finish by about one-fourth inch of dirt dug out of the hole. It should look as if some animal had dug the hole and scratched the dirt out in front. Use a small shovel made for the purpose, or a sharpened stick to dig the hole, and keep your gloves on all the time. Do not walk around, but stand in the same spot until the set is complete. Now put a piece of bait in the back of the hole, using a sharpened stick to handle the bait and put just a little scent by the side of the hole. When you catch a fox, kill him without drawing blood, and set the trap back in the same place. Your chances for catching another fox are doubled. Skunks, coons and other animals will also be caught in these sets.

The following method is a good one to use in settled countries, as it is not so likely to catch dogs and other animals, as other methods are. Find an ant-hill, a small, pointed knoll, an old rotten stump, a moss covered rock, or an old log with one end off the ground. Set the trap on the highest point, covering carefully, so that it looks just like it did before the trap was set. Place a fair-sized bait, such as a skunk or muskrat about eight feet away from the trap. The fox is always suspicious of a bait, especially a large one, and will always get on the highest point to look at it before going close. Of course, there must be no other place for him to get up on, near the bait. In the winter, traps may be set on muskrat houses, and bait placed on the ice. I think it best to set the traps several days before placing the baits, as in that way the human and other scents have a chance to pass away. When baiting, go just close enough to throw the bait into place.

200

Some trappers set traps around large baits, such as the carcass of a horse, cow or sheep, but I think it best to place the bait by the side of a trail and set several traps on the trail from thirty to seventy five yards from the bait. When feeding on the bait the foxes will travel on the trail, and they will not be looking for danger so far away from the bait. Comparatively few of the professional fox trappers can trap the fox successfully after the deep snow comes on; but the following methods are the best known, and will catch the fox if you use care in setting. Of course, snow sets of any kind can only be used when the snow is dry and loose and likely to remain in that condition for some time.

The first method given is the one used by the Canadian Indians, for taking the silver fox in the great northern wilderness. Out on the ice on some frozen lake, or on any open, windswept piece of ground, make a cone-shaped mound of snow, beating it solid, so that it will not drift away. The trap should be fastened to a clog, and the clog buried in the mound. Make the mound about two feet high, and make a hollow in the top for the trap to set in. The hollow should be lined with cat-tail down, or some other dry material, and the trap set in the hollow and covered first with a sheet of white note paper, finishing with a half inch or more of loose snow. Do not handle this snow with your hands, for if you do it will be certain to freeze on the trap. The best way is to take a bunch of evergreen boughs, and brush the snow up over the mound so that it sifts lightly over the trap. The covering on the trap should be a little lower than the top of the mound so that the wind will not uncover the trap. The bait is cut into small pieces and stuck into the sides of the mound.

After the trap is set it will only require a short time for the wind to drift your tracks shut and remove all traces of human presence, and the trap will remain in working order as long as the cold weather lasts. If water rises on the ice it will not reach your trap, and if there is a snowstorm, the first wind will blow the loose snow off the mound, leaving just a little over the trap. When looking at the traps you should not go nearer than fifty yards, and do not turn off your route, but walk straight by. This is a splendid method for use in the far north where the snow never melts or freezes during the winter months. Scent is more used for fox trapping than for trapping any other animal. One of the best scents known for dry land or water sets is prepared as follows: Remove the fat from one or two skunks, chop it fine, and take a sufficient quantity to almost fill an ordinary pickle bottle. Take two mice; cut them up and add to the fat and let the bottle stand in the sun until the mixture is thoroughly decomposed; then add the scent of two skunks and five or six muskrats. The bottle must be kept covered so the flies will not blow it, but it must not be tightly corked.

Another very good one is made by allowing the flesh of a muskrat to rot in a bottle, and adding about four ounces of strained honey and one-half ounce of essence of musk. Pure fish oil is attractive to the fox, and is used by some very good trappers. When making blind-sets, or when setting on a trail some distance from a bait, do not stake your traps, but fasten them to a drag of some kind: a brush, a stone or a grapple. By so doing the fox will not spoil the trail for the next one, and the trap may be set back in the same place. For bait set on dry land, the trap may be staked to advantage, for if one fox is caught and rolls around over the ground, you are more likely to catch another one there.

Do not start out with a dozen traps and expect to make a success of fox trapping. You should have all the traps that you can look after.

Do not depend on one method of setting, as a fox will sometimes learn your method, but some other method, even if it is not so good, may fool them.

When killing foxes in traps, do so at every opportunity. If at all possible, do so without drawing blood. One of the best ways is by piercing the heart with a wire dagger. Another good way is by breaking the neck, which may be done as follows: strike the fox a light blow over the head with a stick, just hard enough to slightly stun him, and when he drops down, place your left hand on the back of his neck, pinning him to the ground and with your right hand pull his nose backward against his back. It requires some practice to do this right.

The track of the red fox resembles that of a small dog, being perhaps a trifle narrower. The length of step is about twelve or fourteen inches, and the foot-prints of an average sized fox will measure about one and a half inches in length.

The track of the gray fox is rounder and more like that of a cat.

Some hunters claim that they can distinguish the track of the male fox from that of the female, the footprints of the female being smaller and a trifle narrower in proportion.

There is no difference in the footprints of the black, silver, cross, and red foxes.

Bear

The bear family is a large one, and its members are found scattered over the greater part of the globe, Australia and Africa being excepted. They range through all latitudes, from the equator to the poles. The following species have been described by naturalists: Polar bear, grizzly bear, European Brown bear, American Black bear, Alaskan Brown bear, Inland White bear, Glacier bear of Alaska, Asiatic bear, Siberian bear, Spectacled bear of South America, Tibetan bear, Borneo bear and Malay bear. The three latter are called Sun bears, from their habit of basking in the rays of the mid-day sun. They are the smallest members of the family and live exclusively on vegetables.

Bears differ from each other in consequences of the differences of climate, more than almost any other animal. Those that inhabit the far north and such high, cold regions as the Rocky Mountains, are monsters, of great strength and ferocity, while those that inhabit warm countries are small, feeble, and inoffensive. The smallest of all is the Borneo bear, while the Alaskan Brown bear is probably the largest. The grizzly or silver tip, and the Polar bears are very large.

The American black bear is probably the most numerous of the family, and is one of most interest to the trappers. With the exception of the prairie country, they are found scattered over almost all of the United States, and a large part of Canada and Alaska. The cinnamon is only a color variety of the black bear, differing only in color. Both kinds are found in the same litter. In some sections, as for instance in some of the northwestern states, and in Mexico, the cinnamon bear predominates, while in the east and north they are very rare. The average weight of the Black bear, when full grown, is from two hundred to three hundred pounds, but specimens have been killed weighing far more. The fur is fine and soft and usually of a jet-black color.

Bears of all kinds, with the exception of the Sun bears and the Polar bear, feed on both vegetable and animal food. The Polar bear lives entirely on fish and flesh. Bears, with the exception of the Polar species, hibernate in winter. They usually den in the ground or rocks, but sometimes in a hollow log or tree.

The mating season is in July and August and the young, usually two, are born in January, February and March. They remain with the mother until fall, and sometimes longer.

In areas where they are found in fair numbers, they form trails through passes in the mountains, along the bottoms of the cliffs, around points of the lakes, and in other places of like nature. These trails may be easily distinguished from the paths of other animals, by the marks on the trees. At intervals, all along the trail, the bear will stand on his hind feet, by the side of a tree, gnaw a circle around the tree, about five feet above the ground. I am told that this marking is done during the mating season. The trails are traveled more in the spring and summer than in the fall.

Bears are very fond of fish, and in the North, when fish are in the streams, spawning, the bears spend much of their time fishing, at the foot of the falls. The sucker is the first fish to spawn, and as soon as they are gone, the pike come, and the bears fare well for a couple of weeks. After that they feed on the leaves of the poplar, insects, berries and nuts, and whatever meat they can find. In some sections they remain in the same locality during the entire year; in other places they migrate on the approach of cold weather and do not return until spring.

The bear becomes prime about the first to the fifteenth of November, and remains in good condition until late in the spring. In northern sections they do not commence shedding until June fifteenth, and sometimes even later. The best time to trap them is in the spring just after the snow is gone, but many are trapped in the fall.

The most common method for trapping bears is the following: Make a sort of enclosure of old logs, brush, etc., in the form of a V, about eight feet long and two or three feet wide at the entrance. It should be three feet high, behind, but it is not necessary to have it so high in front. The bait should be fastened in the back of the pen, and the trap set in the entrance. Take a small, springy stick, about eight inches long, and spring it under the pan of the trap, to prevent small animals from being caught. To do this, stick one end firmly in the ground, and bend the other end down, and hook it under the pan. The trap when set, should support a weight of twenty-five pounds, but it is my opinion that most trappers allow the trap to spring too easily.

Always turn the loose jaw up, and work from in under, for the sake of safety. Now drive down a couple of stakes on each side of the trap, so as to leave only a narrow passage; cover the trap with leaves or moss. It is a good idea to put a good sized piece of moss over the pan. To cause the bear to step in the center of the trap, some trappers put sharp sticks around the outside of the jaws, others lay a stick across the mouth of the pen, about six or eight inches high, and close up to the jaws. In stepping over it, the bear is more likely to put his foot in the trap. The trap should be fastened to a heavy clog of hardwood. For the Black bear, the clog should be about six or seven feet long, and just small enough to go through the ring on the chain. The ring should be slipped on to the middle and fastened with a spike. For the grizzly and other large bears, the clog should be larger.

This is the best method, but if you nip a bear once, you will have to try some other method, and it is not likely that you will catch him, even then, as they become very cunning. Do not set the trap at the same place, but find his trail, and make a blind set; preferably where the trail leads through a pool of water. Of course you must be sure that no person will travel on the trail. Some trappers prefer to hang the bait about six feet above the trap and do not use any pen.

Bears may also be trapped successfully with snares and deadfalls but the objection to these traps is that the animal is killed instantly and if the traps are not visited daily, the skin is likely to spoil.

For bait, there is nothing better than fish, but pork, mutton, beef or any kind of large game is good. Even the flesh of the bear makes fair bait. Beaver, otter or muskrat meat is also good. Honey is very attractive.

The track of the bear is easily distinguished from that of other animals, because of its large size. Ordinarily, the bear's mode of locomotion is a shuffling walk. The footprints of a large black bear will measure about eight inches in length.

However successful the trapper might have been in taking animals, he would not secure the full reward for his labor unless he knew how to take care of the skins.

Skins that have been riddled with shot find little favor with the dealers; neither do skins that have been cut in stripping off, or that are encumbered with remnants of flesh, or that have become putrefied before drying, or that have been incorrectly stretched, or that have been dried too fast, or that have been neglected and exposed after being cured. Great quantities of valuable furs are rendered nearly worthless by bad treatment in the process of preservation. So:

- Be careful to visit your traps often, so that the skins will not have time to become spoiled.
- As soon as possible after an animal is dead and dry, attend to the skinning and curing.
- Scrape off all superfluous flesh and fat but be careful not to go so deep as to cut the fiber of the skin.
- Don't dry a skin by fire or directly in the sun, but rather in a cool shady place, sheltered from the rain.
- In drying skins it is important that they should be stretched tight, as though on a drum-head.

There are two ways of skinning fur-bearing animals: *casing* and skinning *open*. The weasel, mink, marten, fisher, fox, opossum, muskrat, civet, skunk, wildcat should be cased.

The raccoon, bear, beaver, badger, cougar, wolf, wolverine, and coyote should be skinned open.

To *case* a skin, cut it loose around the feet and rip down the back of the hind legs, to and around the vent.

Peel the skin carefully from the hind legs and skin the tail by slipping a split stick over the bone, Then grip the stick with the right hand, holding the bone of the tail between the second and third fingers, draw the skin downward from the body, keeping it as clean of flesh and fat as possible. To facilitate this process the animal may be suspended from the limb of a tree or other projection by looping a strong cord around the hind legs after they have been skinned. The skin should be drawn from the front legs and when the ears are reached they should be cut off, cutting downwards towards the head. The skin should be cut loose about the eyes and nose, and it will then be in the form of a long pocket, fur side in.

The weasel, mink, marten, fisher, fox, skunk, civet cat, and wild cat should be skinned in this way. The otter must have the tail ripped open its entire length on the underside, and as they are a difficult animal to flesh, it is best to skin them clean with a knife, leaving no flesh or fat adhering to the skin. The muskrat and opossum should also be cased, but as the tails of these animals have no fur they should not be skinned, the skin being cut loose about the base or where the fur ends.

To skin an animal *open,* cut the skin on the belly from the point of the lower jaw to the vent, down the back of the hind legs and on the inside of the front legs across the breast to the point of the brisket. Animals that are intended only as furs may have the feet cut off, but bears, mountain lions, wolves and wolverines should have the feet skinned out to the ends of the toes, leaving the claws attached to the skin. The skin should be peeled from the body, using the knife whenever necessary.

In skinning the beaver, rip the skin from the point of the chin to the vent and around the base of the tail and cut off the feet, but do not rip the skin of the legs. Skin the animal perfectly clean using the knife everywhere, as it is a really big job to flesh a beaver after skinning. No flesh or fat should be allowed to remain on the skin.

After all burrs, lumps of mud and blood clots have been removed from the skin it is ready for fleshing. For fleshing all cased skins prepare a narrow tapering board of sufficient length to accommodate the longest skins and plane it perfectly smooth, rounding the edges slightly. Draw the skin over this board flesh side out and scrape all flesh and fat from it, using some blunt instrument, such as a square edged knife or a hatchet. Turn the skin occasionally and do not flesh on the edges of the board or you may score the skin; be careful not to damage it in any way. Always turn the fur side out before laying it down, so as to keep it perfectly clean.

Open skins, if they have not been skinned clean, are more readily fleshed after they are stretched.

A good supply of stretching boards of various sizes should be made in advance of the trapping season. Soft pine, poplar, basswood, or cedar boards are best. They should be free of knots and should be planed smooth so that the furs may be removed easily after they are dry.

For mink the boards should be from 26 to 34 inches in length and from 3 ½ to 4 ½ inches wide at the widest part, and about ½ inch narrower at the shoulders from which point it should taper to the head and end with a rounded point. For marten, the boards should be a trifle wider.

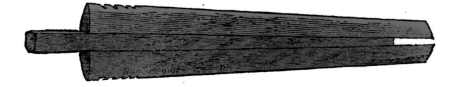

For the average fox or fisher, the board should be 4 feet long, about 5 ¼ inches wide at the shoulder and 6 ½ at the base.

For the otter the board should be about ½ inch wider and a foot longer.

The average lynx will require a board about 7 ½ inches wide at the shoulder and 9 and 1 ½ inches at the base, by about 5 feet in length.

For large muskrats the board should be two feet long by 6 inches wide at the base, ¾ inches narrower at the shoulder and with a flat iron shaped head, but more rounded at the nose.

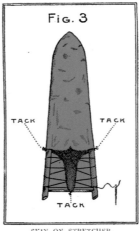

SKIN ON STRETCHER.

One should have several smaller sizes also. For skunk and opossum the boards should be about 6 inches wide at the shoulder and 7 ¼ inches at the base, 28 inches long. These dimensions are for the average animals, but it should be remembered that the sizes vary greatly. In the case of the skunk and the mink especially, there is a great difference in size.

All boards should be beveled on the sides, leaving the edges thin, round and smooth.

The skins should be stretched as soon as they are fleshed.

The proper way to stretch *open* skins is by lacing them with twine in a hoop or frame.

The beaver should be stretched round, and a hoop is most convenient. Fasten the skin in the hoop at four points and then with a large sacking needle and strong twine stretch out one quarter at a time. Use a separate twine for each quarter, sewing thru the edge of the skin and around the hoop, tying the end with a loose knot. If any part is stretched too much or not enough, it is a simple matter to untie the string and give it a little slack or take up a little.

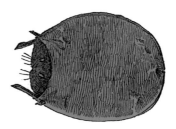

The raccoon should be stretched nearly square and all other skins to their natural shape. A square frame is most convenient, and the method employed is the same as for beavers. Open skins which have not been fleshed, should have all of the flesh peeled off after they are stretched though it will often be necessary to re-stretch them. But this is not difficult. All furs should be dried or cured in a cool, airy place. They should never be allowed near the heat of the fire as they dry rapidly and become brittle. In camp they may be dried in some corner, removed from the fire but they are likely to take on a dirty yellow color from the smoke, and it is better to have a shelter for them on the outside.

Furs should not be allowed to remain a long time on the boards. As soon as they are sufficiently dry to prevent shrinking or wrinkling they should be removed. The lynx and all varieties of foxes should be turned with the fur side out as soon as they become dry enough. If the skin has become too dry to turn, it may be dampened slightly on the stiffer parts. A very little time will suffice. Be certain to allow the skin to dry out thoroughly after turning. It is best to watch the skins closely and not allow them to become too dry before turning.

Some trappers turn the skins of other animals, but not counting the above exceptions, it is better to leave the fur side in.

When shipping the pelts they should be packed flat and bound tightly. Those having the fur side out should be kept separate from the others so that the fur will not become greasy.

TRAILING—INDIAN SAGACITY BY RANDOLPH MARCY

I know of nothing in the woodman's education of so much importance, or so difficult to acquire, as the art of trailing or tracking men and animals. To become adept at this art requires the constant practice of years, and with some men a lifetime does not suffice to learn it.

Almost all the Indians whom I have met with are proficient in this species of knowledge, the faculty for acquiring which appears to be innate with them. Exigencies of woodland and prairie-life stimulate him from childhood to develop faculties so important in the arts of war and of the chase.

This difficult branch of woodcraft cannot be taught from books, it is almost always a matter of practice, yet I will give some facts relating to the habits of thinking of the Indian I have known that may facilitate its acquirement.

An Indian, on coming to a trail, can generally tell at a glance its age, by what particular tribe it was made, the number of the party, and many other things connected with it astounding to the uninitiated.

I remember, upon one occasion, as I was riding with a Delaware upon the prairies, we crossed the trail of a large party of Indians traveling with lodges. The tracks appeared to me quite fresh, and I remarked to the Indian that we must be near the party. "Oh no," said he, "the trail was made two days before, in the morning," at the same time pointing with his finger to where the sun would be at about 8 o'clock. Then, seeing that my curiosity was excited to know by what means he arrived at this conclusion, he called my attention to the fact that there had been no dew for the last two nights, but that on the previous morning it had been heavy. He then pointed out to me some spears of grass that had been pressed down into the earth by the horses' hoofs, upon which the sand still adhered, having dried on, thus clearly showing that the grass was wet when the tracks were made.

213

At another time, as I was traveling with the same Indian, I discovered upon the ground what I took to be a bear-track, with a distinctly-marked impression of the heel and all the toes. I immediately called the Indian's attention to it, at the same time flattering myself that I had made quite an important discovery, which had escaped his observation. The fellow remarked with a smile, "Oh no, captain." He then pointed with his gun-rod to some spears of grass that grew near the impression, but I did not comprehend the mystery until he dismounted and explained to me that, when the wind was blowing, the spears of grass would be bent over toward the ground, and the oscillating motion thereby produced would scoop out the loose sand into the shape I have described. The truth of this explanation was apparent, yet it occurred to me that its solution would have baffled the wits of most white men.

Fresh tracks generally show moisture where the earth has been turned up, but after a short exposure to the sun they become dry. If the tracks be very recent, the sand may sometimes, where it is very loose and dry, be seen running back into the tracks, and by following them to a place where they cross water, the earth will be wet for some distance after they leave it. The droppings of the dung from animals are also good indications of the age of a trail. It is well to remember whether there have been any rains within a few days, as the age of a trail may sometimes be conjectured in this way. It is very easy to tell whether tracks have been made before or after a rain, as the water washes off all the sharp edges.

It is not a difficult matter to distinguish the tracks of American horses from those of Indian horses, as the latter are never shod; moreover, they are much smaller.

In trailing horses, there will be no trouble while the ground is soft, as the impressions they leave will then be deep and distinct; but when they pass over hard or rocky ground, it is sometimes a very slow and troublesome process to follow them. Where there is grass, the trace can be seen for a considerable time, as the grass will be trodden down and bent in the direction the party has moved; should the grass have returned to its upright position, the trail can often be distinguished by standing upon it and looking ahead for some

214

distance in the direction it has been pursuing; the grass that has been turned over will show a different shade of green from that around it, and this often marks a trail for a long time.

Should all traces of the track be obliterated in certain localities, it is customary with the Indians to follow on in the direction it has been going for a time, and it is quite probable that in some place where the ground is more favorable it will show itself again. Should the trail not be recovered in this way, they search for a place where the earth is soft, and make a careful examination, embracing the entire area where it is likely to run. Indians who find themselves pursued and wish to escape, scatter as much as possible, with an understanding that they are to meet again at some point in advance, so that, if the pursuing party follows any one of the tracks, it will invariably lead to the place of rendezvous. If, for example, the trail points in the direction of a mountain pass, or toward any other place which affords the only passage through a particular section of country, it would not be worthwhile to spend much time in hunting it, as it would probably be regained at the pass.

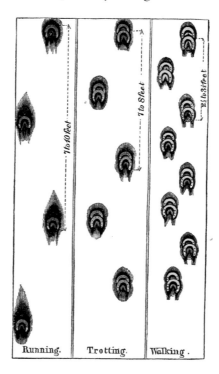

As it is important in trailing Indians to know at what gaits they are traveling, and as the appearance of the tracks of horses are not familiar to all, I have in the above cut represented the prints made by the hoofs at the ordinary speed of the walk, trot, and gallop, so that the person, in following the trail, may form an idea as to the probability of overtaking them, and regulate his movements accordingly.

In traversing a district of unknown country where there are no prominent landmarks, and with the view of returning to the point of departure, a pocket compass should always be carried, and attached by a string to a button-hole of the coat, to prevent its being lost or mislaid; and on starting out, as well as frequently during the trip, to take the bearing, and examine the appearance of the country when facing toward the starting-point, as a landscape presents a very different aspect when viewing it from opposite directions. There are few white men who can retrace their steps for any great distance unless they take the above precautions in passing over an unknown country for the first time; but with the Indians it is different; the sense of locality seems to be innate with them, and they do not require the aid of the magnetic needle to guide them.

Upon a certain occasion, when I had made a long march over an unexplored section, and was returning upon an entirely different route without either road or trail, a Delaware, by the name of "Black Beaver," who was in my party, on arriving at a particular point, suddenly halted, and, turning to me, asked if I recognized the country before us. Seeing no familiar objects, I replied in the negative. He put the same question to the other white men of the party, all of whom gave the same answers, whereupon he smiled, and in his quaint vernacular said, "Injun he don't know nothing. Injun big fool. White man mighty smart; he know heap." At the same time he pointed to a tree about two hundred yards from where we were then standing, and informed us that our outward trail ran directly by the side of it, which proved to be true.

This same Black Beaver would start from any place to which he had gone by a sinuous route, through an unknown country, and keep a direct bearing back to the place of departure; and he assured me that he has never, even during the most cloudy or foggy weather, or in the darkest nights, lost his sense of direction.

I have known several men, after they had become lost in the mountains, to wander about for days without exercising the least judgment, and finally exhibiting a state of mental aberration almost upon the verge of lunacy. Instead of reasoning upon their situation, they exhaust themselves running ahead at their utmost speed without any regard to direction.

When a person is satisfied that he has lost his way, he should stop and reflect upon the course he has been traveling, the time that has elapsed since he left his camp, and the probable distance that he is from it; and if he is unable to retrace his steps, he should keep as nearly in the direction of them as possible; and if he has a compass, this will be an easy matter; but, above all, he should guard against following his own track around in a circle with the idea that he is in a beaten trace.

When he is traveling with a train of wagons which leaves a plain trail, he can make the distance he has traveled from camp the radius of a circle in which to ride around, and before the circle is described he will strike the trail. If the person has no compass, it is always well to make an observation, and to remember the direction of the wind at the time of departure from camp; and as this will not generally change during the day, it would afford a means of keeping the points of the compass.

In the night Ursa Major (the Great Bear) is not only useful to find the north star, but its position, when the pointers will be vertical in the heavens, may be estimated with sufficient accuracy to determine the north even when the north star cannot be seen. In tropical latitudes, the zodiacal stars, such as Orion, give the east and west bearing, and the Southern Cross the north and south when Polaris and the Great Bear cannot be seen.

FINDING YOUR WAY—THE SUN BY ELMER HARRY KREPS

There are ways of discovering direction without a compass that may be used to good advantage. First there is the sun. In theory it rises in the east and sets in the west; but in reality it only behaves so on or very near the equator. As we are in the northern hemisphere the sun is of course south of the east— west line all the time, and in winter it is even farther south than in summer.

In consequence, the sun rises somewhat south of the east in summer and sets a little south of west. In winter it rises still farther south and its path across the sky is always to the south of us. At noon it is straight south. So if one knows approximately the time of day he can easily figure out the compass points.

HOW TO USE YOUR WATCH AS A COMPASS

Directions by the sun can be learned with even more accuracy—if one has a watch—because knowing the time of day exactly, he should know just how far the sun is from the zenith at that time and thus easily locate the true south. Having found it, he has but to face in that direction and the north will then be behind him, the east on his left and the west on his right side.

But there is an even better way of finding direction using a watch. Holding the watch so that the hour hand points to a line perpendicular to the sun, count half way from this hour to twelve and this will be south; in other words half way between the hour hand and the figure twelve is south. Count forward from the hour hand to twelve in the forenoon, but in the afternoon the south is half way between the hour hand and twelve, counting back towards twelve.

THE WATCH AS A COMPASS.

The drawing conveys the idea more clearly. The time shown is 8 p.m. and with the hour hand pointed towards the sun; south would be midway between 8 and 12 or in line with the figure 10.

When the sun is invisible and no compass or other ordinary means of locating directions is available it is advisable to stay in camp if possible. But it is well to know means of finding directions under such conditions for one never knows what may happen and a little knowledge along this line can do no harm even if it is never used. We sometimes read or hear from woodsmen of such means and usually they are given as safe and reliable methods. But they should never be taken too seriously. For instance we are told that moss grows only on the north side of trees, while the larger branches are on the south side. This is true in a general way but conditions have their effect and the shelter of the other trees or nearby hills may reverse the order more or less. But the fact that the sun's rays never directly reach the north side of a tree encourages the growth of moss on that side, while the almost constant sunshine by day, on the south side, causes the sap to flow there more vigorously and thus gives a greater growth to the branches on the south side. In prairie country the prevailing wind, usually from the north, will give a permanent incline to the grass, which may help one to locate directions.

TRACKS, FOR THE TRAPPER

Experienced trappers can read the signs of forest and stream with a degree of accuracy that to the rest of us is surprising. He can make a fair estimate of the number and kinds of fur-bearing animals found in a locality, while the novice would see nothing.

It's essential for successful hunting and trapping to be able to read the signs accurately. The experienced trapper will know instantly, on seeing a track, just what animal it was that passed that way and—by knowing its habits—will know about when it is likely to return, and how to place a trap for its capture. He can also tell with fair accuracy at what time the animal passed that way, and frequently, will know whether it was a male or female; whether it was looking for food or a place of rest, whether it was on its regular route of travel, and where it was going.

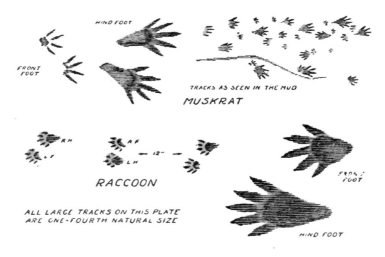

HIND FOOT

FRONT FOOT

TRACKS AS SEEN IN THE MUD

MUSKRAT

RACCOON

ALL LARGE TRACKS ON THIS PLATE ARE ONE-FOURTH NATURAL SIZE

FRONT FOOT

HIND FOOT

Before the coming of the tell-all snow, and the myriad tracks that then appear, the stream with its muddy or sandy shores is the most promising place to look for signs. In the mud alongside of a pool of water, the tracks of that busy little animal the muskrat can be seen. When it is seen at the water's edge—and only a few tracks are visible—the trail appears irregular. But if one can see where it has walked for some distance, it will be seen that the animal has a regular step, some five or six inches in length. There is also the trail of the dragging tail, most plainly seen in the soft muddy bottom of the still, shallow water. In the snow the track will appear the same. But only the prints of the hind feet are visible, the front feet being very much smaller, and the print being obliterated by those of the hind feet. When the animal is running the prints of all four feet are readily discernible. The print of the hind foot will measure about two and a fourth inches in length if the full impression of the foot is to be seen.

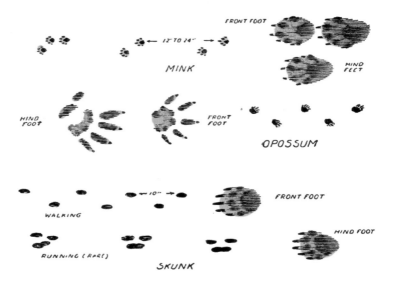

The trail of the otter is unmistakable, owing to its peculiar, floundering, sliding mode of travel. It is seldom seen except in the near vicinity of the water. In the snow, the track is well defined and resembles the trail made by dragging a small log, the footprints in the bottom of the trail being very distinct. The length of jump is from four to eight feet, depending on the condition of the snow, and the footprints will measure about two inches in diameter.

Another animal that frequents the waterways is the mink. The track of this little animal may be found along the muddy shore, where the steep bank crowds it down to the water's edge. At other times it will travel some distance from the water, and after the ice forms, will run on the ice, seldom

222

going far from the shore. Its method of travel is an easy lope, and the footprints are nearly always in pairs about three inches apart, one somewhat in advance of the other, and separated by a distance of from one to two feet. The footprints measure from one to one and three-fourths inches in length. They are sometimes found entering the water at spring holes in the ice, and at open places in the rapids.

TRACKS, FOR THE HUNTER

While deer are not classed among the fur-bearing animals, they are interesting to all trappers, Note the drawings of the footprints of the common deer, the moose, the caribou, and the three most common species of rabbits, namely; the common cottontail, the snowshoe rabbit, and the jack rabbit. The tracks shown in one-fifth size are of the cottontail.

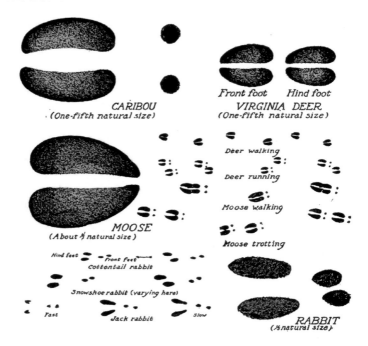

CARIBOU
(One-fifth natural size)

Front foot   Hind foot
VIRGINIA DEER
(One-fifth natural size)

Deer walking

Deer running

Moose walking

MOOSE
(About ⅛ natural size)

Moose trotting

Hind feet   Front feet
Cottontail rabbit

Snowshoe rabbit (varying hare)

Fast   Jack rabbit   Slow

RABBIT
(⅛ natural size)

As you see in the drawings of the deer tracks, the hind foot is narrower and more pointed than that of the front. The doe also makes a smaller and more slender track. The average track will measure about two and a fourth inches in length.

The moose makes a similar track, but it is much larger and will measure about four and a half to five and a half inches.

The track of the caribou will average somewhat smaller than that of the moose and is of wholly different shape. It is not so pointed, and the hoof is split much higher, and it spreads out more. Also the prints of the two small toes on the back

224

of the foot are to be seen in nearly all cases, while the moose does not always show them.

Almost everybody is familiar with the track of the rabbit, but we have shown three species, mainly to show the difference in their size. The feet being furred heavily, the prints of the toes seldom show, except on hard snow.

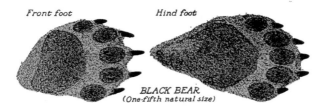

Front foot   *Hind foot*

BLACK BEAR
(One-fifth natural size)

One is unlikely to mistake the track of the bear. It is the largest of the furbearing animals. Its tracks may sometimes be seen in the mud and wet moss of the northern swamps, also on the shores of the lakes and along the streams.

The bear has a shuffling gait and turns its toes outward. It is fond of walking on logs and will do so frequently, where fallen timber is plentiful. The track of a large black bear will sometimes measure eight inches in length, and that of the grizzly bear will be much larger.

Even when the beaver market collapsed in the 1840s, and after the last great meet-ups, the mountains still beckoned. Now the trappers of earlier days found work as army scouts, hunters for mining companies (and later for railroads), and as guides for the great wagon train migrations.

And today, because the mountains still beckon—as they have always beckoned—the mountain man works as a Hunting or Mountain Guide, a Game Warden, Mining Engineer, Forest Ranger, Logger, and Smoke Jumper.

The Rendezvous, as every devotee of the ethos of the mountain man knows, was the yearly meet-up of the trappers and traders, company men and independents, families, friends and hangers-on. It took place in high summer, well after the trapping season had ended.

Perhaps Neihardt in *A Splendid Wayfaring* described it best:

> Ten weeks had elapsed since Ashley's party had separated into four bands and struck out in as many directions from the camp on the Green River fifteen mile above the Sandy's mouth; and now all the trappers employed by Ashley in that country, including the parties of Smith and Sublette who had wintered west of the divide, began to arrive at the place of rendezvous, their pack-animal laden with the precious spoils of many a beaver stream. By the 1st of July, 1825, one hundred and twenty men, including the twenty-nine who had deserted from the Hudson Bay Company, were encamped on the Green at the mouth of Henry's Fork. Beckwourth tells us that many of the Frenchmen had their squaws and children with them, and that the encampment was "quite a little town."
>
> When all had come in, the General opened his goods, "consisting of flour, sugar, coffee, blankets, tobacco,

whisky, and all other articles necessary for that region." Whereupon, so Beckwourth assures us, the jubilee began. Some of these men had left St. Louis with Henry in the spring of 1822 and had been in the wilderness ever since. Many had not tasted sugar or coffee for many months, having lived entirely on the game of the country, and tobacco and whisky were luxuries not to be despised. These articles were purchased at enormous prices, and many a trapper not only swallowed in a day of ease what he had earned in a year of constant danger and hardship, but when the rendezvous broke up found himself indebted to his employer for his next year's outfit. Storytelling, gambling, drinking, feasting, horse-racing, wrestling, boxing and target-shooting were the order of the day, "all of which were indulged in with a heartiness that would astonish more civilized societies," says Beckwourth.

The free trappers, who were not paid by the year as were the hired trappers, but, being their own masters, trapped where they pleased and sold their furs at the annual rendezvous, were the "cocks of the walk." These boasted freely with naivete of children—or Homeric heroes. As Joseph Meek tells us: "They prided themselves on their hardihood and courage; even on their recklessness and profligacy. Each claimed to own the best horses; to have had the wildest adventures; to have made the most narrow escapes; to have killed the greatest number of bears and Indians; to be the greatest favorite with the Indian belles; to be the greatest consumer of alcohol; and to have

the most money to spend—that is, the largest credit on the books of the company. If his hearers did not believe him, he was ready to run a race with them, to beat them at 'cold sledge,' or to fight, if fighting were preferred—ready to prove what he affirmed in any way the company pleased."

While this orgy proceeds, the year's business is transacted.

The classic or golden age of the mountain man lasted for about a generation: from 1810, when Americans began to get themselves organized to take advantage of the natural resources the Louisiana Purchase had made available—particularly the abundant and portable beaver pelt—until about 1840. By then the beaver boom had pretty much ended, and that same year saw the last great Rendezvous up on the Green River in what is now Wyoming.

These days the memory of those lives and times is kept alive by the many Mountain Man re-enactors who yearly rendezvous out west. Like the trappers and traders of olden days, they meet-up to buy and sell, to gossip and tell tall tales, to engage in tests of strength and skill, and to party. Their aim is to live, if just for a few days, the lives of those by-gone American—I don't think I exaggerate—heroes. There is something almost mystical in their total immersion in the dress, and tools and guns—in short, the way of the Mountain Man. And I fancy they hear—when the noise and bustle of camp has quieted and the fire has burned low—whispers, of that other time.

"And now suddenly there was nothing but a world of cloud, and we three were there alone in the middle of a great white plain with snowy hills and mountains staring at us; and it was very still; but there were whispers."

—"Black Elk," *Black Elk Speaks*, by John G. Neihardt